RAISING THE BAR

A Higher Standard for Team Leadership

— Ron Bernard

Copyright ©2016 Ron Bernard
Cover Design by For Creative Sake

ENDORSEMENTS

This is a must read for those desiring a "new way" to do effective team leadership in ministry as well as in the corporate world. The peer-level leadership team promotes a higher standard of leadership based on the idea that together everyone accomplishes more. Ron has been gifted with powerful insight into how this type of leadership team functions through first-hand experience. And the good news is he is making it available to you. We highly recommend this book as an excellent resource to all leaders who are looking for answers.

    –Larry and Janet Bowen, Pastors
    Life Giving Church
    Woodward, OK

The character of a man is measured by how he stands in moments of challenge and controversy, whether he responds with grace or reacts with grit. <u>Raising the Bar</u> *answers more than just the "How To" of leadership, it also answers the question of "Who!" In an age where "Gifting and Charisma" have dominated and "Character" has acquiesced, this book will turn the reader's attention back to the "Standard" of Church leadership: GODLY CHARACTER. Through the crucibles, the furnaces, and successes of his own leadership walk, Ron has captured the humility necessary for making Godly Character the vehicle for all gifting. A must read for this generation of budding leaders within the Church.*

    —Michael Pedersen, Pastor
    Fountain of Life Church
    Regina, Saskatchewan, Canada

Some of my earliest memories of church life are attending conferences at Ron's church in Texas. Throughout my life I have known him to be a lover of Jesus and his church. I have been privileged to learn from him and work alongside him as a mentor and friend. Ron's desire for the church to come into maturity is very evident. He is a Kingdom minded man with great insights into scripture and the desire to see those truths practically implemented and functioning in the lives of every believer and every church. I have no doubt that this book will be a blessing to you and equip you to walk more closely with the Lord.

    —Daniel Matthews, Associate Pastor
        Family of Faith Church
        Director of Student Ministry
        Family of Faith College
        Shawnee, OK

If you need a book that takes you to another level in leading your team, training your team, or even shifting the way you think and respond to team I want to recommend Ron's book, <u>Raising the Bar</u>. Having read the book I find it so practical and yet so in tune with what God is doing in this hour. Sometimes authors get so deep that they end up destroying truth but Ron's simple approach takes every reader into a journey that will transform the way they lead. Having traveled to many countries over the years I find these insights pertinent and necessary if there is going to be growth in any area of ministry in which someone leads. All I can say is get the book.

    ---Dr. Bennett C. Smith
        President, On Track International - The Dream Conference
        Senior Pastor/Bishop - Legacy Church International
        Mobile, Alabama

IT'S WHAT'S INSIDE THAT COUNTS

FIRST WORDS: *Raising the Bar* – p.6

Chapter 1: *Not Your Everyday, Run-of-the-Mill Team* – p.7

Chapter 2: *What Does "Team" Mean?* – p.10

Chapter 3: *What's So Good About It?* – p.22

Chapter 4: *Counting the Cost* – p.29

Chapter 5: *Making it Work* – p.40

Chapter 6: *Before You Say "I Do"* – p.51

Chapter 7: *Follow the Leader* – p.58

Chapter 8: *Is He Worth Following?* – p.65

Chapter 9: *Are They Worth Leading?* – p.79

Chapter 10: *Foundation Stones* – p.91

Chapter 11: *Putting it Together and Keeping it Together* – p.102

Chapter 12: *Where the Rubber Meets the Road* – p.108

LAST WORDS: *It's Not Just "Pie in the Sky"* – p.111

ACKNOWLEDGEMENTS – p.112

FIRST WORDS
Raising the Bar

The gold medal in the high jump competition during the 1968 Olympic Games in Mexico City was won by an American named Dick Fosbury who set a new Olympic record when he cleared the bar at 7 feet, 4¼ inches. His innovative style of jumping over the bar "backwards" became known as the Fosbury Flop, and it quickly became the style that almost all high-jumpers have been using, in one form or another, since then. The new standard that he established in high jumping styles literally resulted in raising the bar in his sport.

I believe that it is time for a "raising of the bar" when it comes to team leadership. The concept of team leadership has been around for a long time, but its effectiveness has been hit-and-miss. Sometimes it has worked well, but at other times it has failed miserably. What I am presenting here is a higher standard that will allow you to achieve excellence in team leadership. Although many of the principles presented here have been applied to some degree in most team settings (and with some positive results), I am convinced that a team will become truly successful only when it applies ALL of these principles to the way it functions. If you truly want your team to be the best it can possibly be, read on!

And as you read through this book, please understand that I believe that both men and women are called to be leaders and/or members of peer-level teams, but I have chosen to use masculine pronouns in the generic sense in most places in this book for the sake of easier reading.

Chapter 1
Not Your Everyday, Run-of-the-Mill Team

Several years ago when I was talking with a friend of mine in Mexico, he told me that, in his opinion, the reason the Mexican national soccer team had never won the world cup was because it always recruited players who had great skills, but each one wanted to be the "star." Therefore, it was impossible to get them to consistently play together as a team because each one wanted the glory and recognition for himself. Their teams did have many excellent players over the years, and they won a lot of games, but when it came down to the really important games, other teams recognized this weakness in them and used it to their advantage, thereby defeating Mexico whenever it mattered the most. However, things were obviously different for the team Mexico sent to the 2012 Olympics. This group of players understood that they would have to work together as a team in order to win it all, and indeed they did win the gold that year. This team also had excellent players, but the difference that year was that each player was willing to put the good of the team ahead of his own personal desire for fame and glory.

The importance of the team concept first hit home for me when I was a student at Phillips University in Enid, Oklahoma. Phillips was a Christian university affiliated with the Disciples of Christ denomination, and as such had, from its beginning, decided that it would not allow fraternities and sororities on campus. Instead, there were several social/service clubs for the students to join if they so desired. By the time I arrived on campus, those clubs had evolved to the point that there was generally a little more emphasis on the social than on the service aspect, so they were a lot like fraternities and sororities but without their own houses.

In the spring semester of my freshman year I decided to pledge (become a Squire) with the Knights of Camelot Club. I chose this one over the others because I loved the idea of knights in shining armor, chivalry, rescuing damsels in distress, honoring God (in those days we were known as the "God Squad" because so many of us were religion majors), and everything else that went along with it. What can I say? I was an idealistic romantic!

One of the things I really enjoyed about being a Knight of Camelot was competing with the other clubs in intramural sports like flag football, basketball, fast-pitch softball, and volleyball. We usually fielded some pretty decent teams, and we occasionally won a championship, but rarely in volleyball because the other clubs usually had taller players who could block and spike the ball really well. One year, however, was different, not because we had great players, but because we put together a team of individuals who understood each other's strengths and weaknesses and who drew upon those strengths and then covered for the weaknesses in each other. We had some who were good at spiking and blocking, some who were too short for that but were really good at "digging out" a spiked ball or diving for a ball to keep it in play, some who were great at setting up a spike, and some who were excellent with the serve. So we set up our rotation to allow each person to utilize his greatest strengths as much as possible, and then we supported him in that position with lots of praise and encouragement. The members of the team we fielded that year were, overall, shorter than those on every other team we played against, but we won the championship by working together as a team!

I learned then that it takes a **special kind of** team to see fulfillment of the dreams carried by that team! Not just any kind of "team" can achieve its goals. There must be a higher standard to aim for! The bar must be raised! Many books have been written about the importance of teamwork, but few, if any, have approached the concept of team in the way that I am presenting it here.

Think about it for a minute. Just how successful are you in what you are doing? Is your business the best it can be? Is your ministry accomplishing everything for which it was begun? Is the team you are coaching reaching its full potential? If not, why not? Maybe it is because you either have no leadership team around you or because what you have is the wrong kind of team. Everything that you are doing can be more successful than it is right now if you are willing to work with the right kind of team.

Chapter 2
What Does "Team" Mean?

At the mention of the word "team," most people automatically think about one or more of their favorite sports teams. In the NFL my favorite teams are the Dallas Cowboys and the Denver Broncos. In college football I like the Oklahoma Sooners and the Aggies of Texas A&M. In MLB it's the Texas Rangers and the Colorado Rockies. I enjoy watching other sports, but I don't really have any favorites that I follow. I know that others have their own favorites, and that is what makes sports successful; each team has its own fan base. And when people think about their favorite teams, they rarely think first about one individual; instead, they think about a group of individuals, each with his or her own particular talents, working together toward a common goal --- winning games. Of course there are individuals who stand out because of their talents, personalities, or leadership abilities, but these would rarely have become noteworthy if they were not a part of a team.

Even though the word "team" has become closely associated with sports, it should also be a companion to the word "leadership." Leadership should be a team effort. The Bible also supports the concept of team. When God created Adam He said that it was not good for the man to be alone, so He gave him Eve to be a help suitable to him --- the first team. Moses not only had Aaron for his spokesman, but he also had a team of leaders around him that helped carry the load of leading millions of people into their destiny. Jesus had His twelve, Paul had others with him in his travels, and elders (plural) were appointed in each of the churches that Paul started.

While there are obviously those who are "born leaders," no leader is able to accomplish much without having others around him or her. Yet, when leadership teams are mentioned, there are a surprising number of opinions as to what that team should look like. Let's take a look at the most common examples of what is called team leadership.

THE YES-MAN TEAM

I knew a pastor who had been a businessman for a long time before entering the ministry. Following the advice of someone who had many years of experience as a pastor, he placed a team of elders around him who helped him lead the church. At first they all felt like they were able to freely express their opinions and that they were always included in the decision-making process. One day, however, this pastor announced to the elders that he had become very frustrated with doing things that way and that he wanted to run the church like he had run his business --- he would make the decisions, and the elders would do what he said. Obviously, this was met with resistance from the elders because they had become accustomed to a different kind of team relationship. In fact, their resistance was so strong that the pastor decided not to push them in this direction for fear of possible repercussions affecting the whole church. However, it was clear from that point on that the pastor was not happy, and the elders found themselves torn between submission to his style of leadership and pushing to keep things the way they had been. Were the elders being rebellious against the pastor? To some degree they probably were, but they were partially driven in that direction by what the pastor wanted to institute. It was not long afterwards that the team unraveled.

What this pastor wanted was a yes-man team. He did not want to be challenged or second-guessed by those whom he expected to be "under" him in authority; basically, he had a "my way or the highway" mentality. He wanted to be the "boss" who made all the decisions, and he wanted his team to carry out his instructions. This was very frustrating for the team members because they felt like they were being railroaded and bullied into doing what the leader demanded!

The leader of a yes-man team is in reality a dictator. He sees himself as the only one with any real authority, and he expects others to recognize that and to act accordingly. He brings together a team/board of those who will rubber-stamp his vision and agree with all of his decisions, all the while giving the impression that he is a "team player." Sadly, many leaders in every walk of life implement this concept of team leadership. Things are accomplished, and sometimes some very good things, but because the leader sees himself as having unquestioned authority, he has no checks and balances in place to safeguard him and the rest of the team. Eventually, his areas of weakness undermine much or all of the good that has been done.

THE SUPPORT-LEVEL TEAM

George began his ministry in Africa, and things were going well for him there, but at some point he felt that he was to move his ministry to the United States. He had contacts in the States who sponsored him, and they advised him to incorporate his ministry so that everything would be done properly in accordance with the laws of the land. In order to comply with the requirements to form a corporation, he discovered that he would need a board of directors. This was a new challenge for George because he was accustomed to having a one-man operation in which he alone made all of the decisions regarding his ministry. Since he had no family in the States who would be willing to assume the roles of directors without trying to tell him what to do, he chose people for his board who were already his financial supporters and assistants. However, he did not give them any real decision-making authority.

Many times when an alpha personality starts a ministry or a business, he has a very clear vision of where that new entity should go and how it should get there. There is a reluctance on his part to entrust others with any degree of authority which may prevent that organization from reaching the goals that he, as the founder, has established. Yet in order to comply with the laws governing such organizations, he usually has to form some sort of corporation that will be legally recognized and registered with the government. This, of course, requires some type of governing board to be named in the paperwork. Therefore, he usually satisfies this requirement by naming, in addition to himself, a spouse and a family member or close friend or two (depending on how many are required) as his official board. He places people around him who will satisfy the demands of the law while at the same time making sure that these are people who understand that, for all practical purposes, their positions are nothing more than symbolic.

However, if this person is not a complete idiot, he will realize that his vision, if at all significant, is much bigger than he can accomplish by himself, so he will also choose to put together a team of people who are willing to use their respective gifts and talents to support him in the areas where he is limited by time, ability, or an inflated sense of self-importance. These people will generally be given responsibilities to facilitate his vision in areas such as promotion, scheduling, logistics, and administration. He may pay them well and treat them at least as well as he would a family pet, but far be it for any of them to do anything without his approval or, heaven forbid, try to give him any kind of advice regarding anything to do with the organization, even though he may actually call them his leadership team! In reality, all he really wants is a support-level team.

This kind of support-level team is formed for the sole purpose of implementing the vision of a micromanaging head of an organization. As long as each member of this team does his job well, he will continue to be part of the team; if not, he will be replaced with someone who will more willingly or more effectively carry out the responsibilities given him.

By putting this kind of team in place, the micromanaging head can present himself as one who appears to work with a leadership team while he maintains his autonomy and independence. In reality, he does not make himself accountable to anyone. The obvious danger here is that when a person refuses to make himself accountable, his weaknesses (which he probably refuses to acknowledge) will go unchallenged, and they will eventually come back to bite him in the butt, affecting both him personally and the organization in a negative way, perhaps even causing its demise!

Now, I am not saying that it is wrong to have support-level teams in an organization; in fact, wisdom would dictate doing so. In churches and other civic organizations the support-level teams are often called committees. These are usually staffed by volunteers instead of employees, and they are given specific areas of responsibility. The chairman of each committee reports to the pastor or president, and he and his team are expected to perform well in the areas assigned to them.

If these committees answer to various members of a leadership team and not to one supreme leader, they can be a vital part of implementing the vision of that organization. They should not, however, be a replacement for a true leadership team. Having a support-level team instead of a team that is able to give valuable input to the leader is inviting disaster.

THE BOARD OF DEACONS TEAM

The little Baptist church in East Texas had just celebrated its fiftieth anniversary. It had always been a small church, averaging between thirty and fifty people on any given Sunday. All of the former pastors who were still living had been invited to attend the anniversary celebration. There were fifteen of them besides the three who had died since serving in that church. Only one of them actually attended. He had served there for only a short time because it was the first church to hire him after he finished seminary, and he had simply taken that position to gain experience and to use it as a stepping-stone to move on to larger churches. He came back to pay respects to his "roots." Of the remaining fourteen invitees, three had been interim pastors whose time there was only temporary, and they were unable to attend due to prior commitments. Nine were still involved in full-time ministry, but they had no interest in attending because they had worked hard to put their experiences in that church behind them, and they did not want to relive bad memories and possibly re-open old wounds. The other two had left the ministry because of what had happened to them in that church, and they were still bitter about it.

Why had this church gone through so many pastors in its history, and why had so many of those men been deeply wounded by their experiences there? It was because of the Board of Deacons. As is the case in many small rural churches, a group of well-entrenched people were those who actually ran things. If it had been another denomination (or non-denomination, for that matter), this group could have been called Elders or Trustees or some other name, but since it was Baptist they were called Deacons. And although they were "officially" voted into their positions by the congregation, the reality was that nearly everyone in the church was related to at least one of them, and no one dared cross paths with any of them. As a result, they were never voted out of office; they stayed in power for as long as they desired, and they made sure that everything was done the way they wanted it done. The pastors who came and went were merely employees who were kept around as long as they didn't preach anything disagreeable to the Deacons or didn't try to change things from the way they had always been done. The Deacons also felt that it was their duty to make sure the pastor stayed humble, so they paid him as little as possible, and they provided him with a small, run-down house that they called a parsonage. And since he received "free" housing, they expected him to keep the church building and the grounds in good repair and looking nice at all times. Those pastors who weren't fired by the Deacons usually resigned as soon as they found something better, even if it was something far removed from ministry.

A Board of Deacons style team is, in most respects, just the opposite of the Yes-Man team and the Support-Level team. Instead of one person dictating his desires to a group of people, this group of people dictates its collective desires to the pastor, the one who is supposed to be the leader of the church --- they try to make him their yes-man. This kind of team is formed to preserve and protect the vision as they perceive it to be. Their main goal is to make sure things stay the way they have always been, and the pastor they hire is nothing more than a figurehead leader; he has no real authority. When an organization is led by this kind of team, the organization quickly dies, even though it may continue to exist for many years. Whenever change is rejected, there is always decay.

THE GOVERNING BOARD OF DIRECTORS TEAM

Most large corporations (at least in the United States) are governed at the highest level by something called a Board of Directors, Trustees, Governors, or Regents. That organization's bylaws define the Board's powers, duties, and responsibilities; but, generally, the Board's mission is to shape, reshape, expand, and oversee the vision of that corporation. If the corporation has voting members or shareholders, the Board members are usually chosen and/or retained by elections; if it is a non-public corporation, the founder of that organization normally selects the first Board, and from then on the Board chooses its own members.

A title such as Chairman of the Board is bestowed upon the person who is chosen by that board to be the one who chairs the board meetings and represents the Board publicly, as necessary. Beyond that he is usually simply a voting member of the Board who does not even have veto power regarding decisions the rest of the board makes.

The Board then hires a CEO (Chief Executive Officer) to be the person to run the day-to-day operations of the company. In the beginning, this is usually the person who started the business and he will probably also serve as the Chairman of the Board, but if he dies or decides to do something different, the next person chosen is usually someone who has already established him or herself as a natural leader, a visionary, and a good communicator. However, this successor will seldom be given an official seat on the Board, and the authority that accompanies the position of CEO is defined and limited by the official job description which has already been determined by the Board. This guarantees that no single individual hired by the Board will have final authority in any matter; the final authority rests with the Board.

Unless the CEO is a visionary who is greatly influential and a gifted motivator who can convince the Board to make whatever major changes that he feels would be beneficial to the company, he simply becomes a manager and public spokesman for the corporation. The decisions regarding the company's direction are then made behind closed doors, and the CEO puts a public face to those decisions. The world today is changing rapidly, and a large company must be open to change in order to continue to do well. If the Board is made up of people who are progressive, forward-thinking, innovative, and willing to receive input from others, the corporation will usually prosper. If not, then even the most talented CEO will be unable to make the company successful.

Quite often, the only significant difference between the Governing Board of Directors and the Board of Deacons is that one operates in the business world and the other in the church.

THE CO-EQUAL ELDERS TEAM

Sometimes, when a church is in its beginning stages, perhaps primarily because the founders experienced deep wounds at the hands of someone in leadership who abused the authority that was given him, the decision is made that no one person will have final authority in that organization. Instead, a team of elders in which all members of that team are given equal authority is chosen to lead the church. The theory is that this kind of setting will allow each person on the team to freely express himself openly and honestly without fear of rejection or reprisal, and the result will be a more balanced approach to leadership --- government by consensus.

While this may sound good in theory, the practical application is usually a bit more problematic. Things may start out well, but eventually at least one of the following scenarios will most certainly play out:

1. Because unanimous consent is required on all leadership decisions, some important issue that is critical to the success of the church's ministry may fail to be approved because one or two of the elders think that it is not really necessary or that it is a bad idea altogether. Can you imagine what would have happened if a team of co-equal leaders had been given the responsibility to decide whether or not to use the atomic bomb in WWII? A consensus never would have been achieved. There will always be some decisions that must be made which are not agreeable to everyone on the leadership team.

2. Sometimes decisions *are* made regarding certain courses of action that need to be taken, yet those decisions are not carried out in a timely manner. Because the peer-level team's philosophy prevents any one member of the team from taking the primary leadership position on the team, no one has the authority to call for accountability on that issue. Things tend to stagnate, and those who do consistently follow through with their responsibilities become frustrated with those who do not.

3. Frequently, one of the team members will become the de facto leader of that team as the other team members begin to recognize, respect, and respond to those attributes that just naturally come to the surface in that person. The title of team leader or lead elder may never be bestowed upon that person, but for all practical purposes he becomes that and is allowed to have a greater level of authority than the others.

4. Sometimes one of the elders, either because of a personal agenda or because of frustration with the way the team functions, tries to establish himself as the team leader, de facto or otherwise. This is generally met with resistance from most or all of the rest of the team, and the resulting conflict often causes the team to disintegrate.
5. If it manages to maintain its co-equal structure over a long period of time, the team usually becomes less and less pro-active (forward-thinking, progressive, innovative) and more and more reactive, simply trying to sustain a status quo. As a consequence, the organization stagnates and atrophies.

Putting together a team of individuals who are all leaders in their own right without giving one of them the authority to lead that team is nothing less than a recipe for failure.

THERE IS A BETTER WAY

As I stated at the end of "First Words," it takes a special kind of team to achieve the level of excellence that every team should desire. While there may be some good qualities to be found in each of the above examples of what is called team leadership, and while each of them may experience some measure of success, none of them is able to produce the kind of success that it should. You see, success should not be measured by what has been accomplished but by comparing what has been accomplished to what could and should have been accomplished.

Personally, I want to experience the kind of success that I believe the Apostle Paul was referring to when he said in 2Tim.4:7,8a (NIV), "I have fought the good fight, I have finished the race, I have kept the faith. Now there is in store for me the crown of righteousness, which the Lord, the righteous Judge, will award me on that day…" He believed that he had accomplished all that God had desired of him in this life. I believe that the

Lord has a unique plan not only for individuals but also for churches and other organizations that He calls into existence. According to Jer.29:11 (NIV), those plans are meant to cause us to prosper and not to harm us; they are placed there to give us hope for the future. I refuse to be satisfied with a partial realization of those plans; I want to see those plans fulfilled completely! For it to happen in a church or any other God-ordained organization, it is going to take a different kind of leadership team --- one that is formed to confirm, advance, and give life to the vision that God has given it.

AN UNCOMMON PARADIGM

I believe that a peer-level leadership team is the kind of team that has the potential to produce the greatest possible success in any kind of organization, but especially in local churches and other Christian organizations and ministries. This kind of team is a rarity because most leaders are more familiar or comfortable with one of the other types of team leadership that I described earlier. But this really is a better way of doing team!

Allow me to give an overview of what this kind of team looks like:

- In a peer-level leadership team, each member of the team regards the other members as peers. No one sees himself as superior or inferior to anyone else on the team. There is no intimidation felt by, or demonstrated toward, anyone else on the team.
- Yet, there is also a mutually recognized "first" among equals. There must be someone who will take the lead among the rest, and everyone on the team must agree as to whom that person is. Someone must have "final" and "emergency" authority.
- Each member of the team genuinely values the other members of the team, not just for what they contribute, but also for who they are as individuals.

- The team is made up of a proper blend of different strengths and talents, resulting in a more complete and effective leadership package.
- The team dynamic is relationship-based rather than organization-based.
- It is something that God puts together

This is simply an overview. The rest of this book is devoted to exploring this kind of team from many different angles. As it will become obvious, developing this type of team is not something that comes naturally nor is it something that comes easily. It requires a lot of effort put forth by each one on the team, and there are sacrifices required of every member to make it work, but the results are well worth the effort! The peer-level team is the higher standard that will produce excellence in team leadership!

Chapter 3
What's So Good About It?

Probably the first issue that needs to be addressed is why a peer-level team is better than the other applications of team leadership. The benefits of a peer-level team will become obvious as you read through the rest of this book, but these are some of the more significant ones that you will discover.

LEADERSHIP BALANCE

Perhaps the most obvious benefit is that a peer-level team provides a more balanced leadership than the others. How so? Because apart from Jesus there is no such thing as a perfect leader; our humanity limits us. Even the best leader has areas of weakness in his life. While he may be strong in several key areas, he is still lacking in other areas. That is why he needs around him, not only those who are strong in the areas where he is weak, but also those who have similar strengths but express them differently.

In my early days as a Senior Pastor, I knew that I needed others around me to help provide proper leadership for the church, so I chose some excellent men to be my elders. In doing so, however, I made the same innocent mistake that many novice leaders make --- I chose people who were a lot like me (those having similar strengths and weaknesses), probably because I felt more comfortable around them than I did around those who were not like me. What I did not realize until later was that while our shared strengths gave us excellence in those areas, our shared weaknesses opened doors for a lot of problems that could have been avoided had we been of a more diverse mixture of strengths and weaknesses.

When a team is made up of members who carry a variety of gifts and strengths, and when those members are encouraged to relate together on a peer level, the leadership given by this team presents a more complete package; more like the kind of leadership that we see in Jesus.

A SAFE PLACE

Another benefit is that a peer-level team, since it is built on relationships instead of on a set of rules and regulations, provides safety, protection, and security for the team members. In many respects the relationships that the team members have with each other should be like a marriage that is established on covenant love rather than on a marriage contract. The relationship is never perfect, but it deepens through both the good times and the challenging times because of a commitment that is made to each other and that is then proven over the years.

When my wife and I married, one commitment that we made to each other was that, no matter what we went through, divorce would never be a consideration. This gave each of us the security of knowing that neither one would give up and walk away from the marriage in spite of the problems that we would face in our relationship. And, as is true of every marriage, there were many times when that commitment was tested. But because we stayed true to the promise we made to each other and worked through our difficulties instead of bailing out, our relationship grew stronger with every passing year.

Commitment must also be an essential ingredient in a peer-level team setting, a commitment to build strong relationships with each other for the sake of the Kingdom of God. As the relationships deepen and strengthen through the good times and the difficult times, each member of the team comes to understand that the peer-level team is a safe place to be. This security then allows him to freely contribute to the team everything that he has to offer and to let down his defenses and just be himself.

COVERING AND CORRECTION

In a peer-level team relationship each member's blind spots can be covered and corrected by the others on the team. Each of us has blind spots, areas of weakness that we fail to see in ourselves. In a true peer-level team relationship these blind spots become obvious to the other members of the team. Many of these blind spots are relatively insignificant in that they do no harm to anyone else or to the effectiveness of the team, and these are simply covered by the other team members. By "covered" I do not mean that they are covered up but that each person is loved and accepted in spite of the little quirks or idiosyncrasies that we all have but don't like to admit. Remember, 1Peter 4:8 tells us that love covers a multitude of sins.

As for the more significant blind spots, the ones that can potentially harm others and the effectiveness of the team, these can be corrected in a peer-level relationship because, in this setting, each member not only has the liberty to express himself freely and openly, but he also opens himself to correction by the other team members as it becomes necessary. Several years ago a member of the leadership team on which I serve came to me in private and told me that he saw that I had a problem with pride in my life. As I listened to him, I put on a serious face, expressed great concern, and thanked him for being willing to point it out to me. Inwardly, however, I was feeling angry and thinking that he obviously didn't understand why I was the way I was; it wasn't really pride, it was self-confidence! Well, it wasn't long before conviction worked on me, and it became obvious that he was right; I *was* full of pride. In reality, my wife had tried to tell me this several times before, but I was too proud to listen! As a result of his confirmation of what my wife had been telling me, God was able to get through to me and help me make some changes in this area of my life. I would like to be able to say that I no longer have a problem with pride, but I'm afraid that would be a prideful statement! But the correction was given and received because of my involvement with this kind of team.

This kind of covering and correction puts checks and balances in place that benefit everyone on the team and also the organization that it leads. It even helps prevent the leader of the team from damaging the team and the organization because of major weaknesses that may surface in his life. While the team will be faithful to cover his insignificant blind spots, it will also faithfully correct him in the more serious areas.

TEAM – TOGETHER, EVERYONE ACCOMPLISHES MORE

Another benefit to operating as this kind of team is that each member of the team is able to draw from the strengths of the other team members. When a team consists of a group of individuals who have a variety of different gifts and anointing, it not only provides better leadership for the organization, but it also makes each member of the team more effective in his own area of ministry.

This benefit became very obvious to me after I was asked to be a part of the national leadership team for ICLC (International Christian Leadership Connections). This team has each of the five-fold ministry gifts represented (apostle, prophet, evangelist, pastor, and teacher) with a variety of expressions of each gift. Soon after joining this team, I began to notice that my preaching and teaching, both in the church where I was the pastor and in other places where I ministered, began to move to a new level. I know that part of it was because the others on the team inspired the best in me to come out, but there was more to it than that. I found myself ministering under the anointing that accompanies some of the other five-fold gifts. This was a new experience for me, and I soon came to realize that being in this peer-level relationship with the others on the team actually gave me access to some of their gifts and anointing. The relationships developed in a peer-level team allow for an impartation to take place from each member of the team to the others on the team. Each member's anointing and gifts can be accessed, to some degree, by the others on the team. My ministry took on a whole new dimension that I had never experienced before, and I know it was true for the others as well. An acronym for the word TEAM could be Together, Everyone Accomplishes More!

GROWTH AND DEVELOPMENT

A peer-level leadership team also promotes growth and development in the individual team members. As each one on the team finds security in the open and accepting relationship provided by the peer-level team, he then grows in his own gifts and anointing. He is encouraged and challenged by the others on the team to reach his full potential, not only as a person, but also as a significant part of the Kingdom of God. This is especially true for those who are new to the team. Frequently, these new members are relatively young and are still maturing in their callings. As they are incorporated into the team, the more mature members help guide and strengthen them as they are given more and more opportunities to function in their ministries and callings. And this is not only true for those who are new to the team (both those who are still maturing and those who are new to the team yet already mature in their ministries), but also for those who have been a part of the team for some time as they find themselves being given new opportunities to release what God has put in each of them.

This is possible because no one on the team feels threatened by newcomers. Each current member is secure in his own gifts and callings, in who he is in God, and in what his place is on the team. He does not view new members on the team as potential competitors or threats but as those who will help complete the vision of the team and make it even better than it already is!

When this happens on the level of the leadership team, it then flows into every other part of the organization as well, because what is happening with the leadership of any organization tends to be reflected in nearly every other member of that organization. For example, when you walk into a place of business where the employees are unfriendly and not interested in giving you good service, it is probably because the management team is like that. And, conversely, when they are friendly and helpful, you can be sure the key people are also that way. So when an organization is led by a team that encourages growth and development in its members, that same encouragement will be passed along to everyone who is a part of that organization.

NEW LEADERS NURTURED

As I mentioned above, the members of a peer-level team should always be looking for others in that organization who are developing as leaders, and they should seek to mentor them and help them fulfill their God-ordained destinies. As they do so, they should hold with an open hand those whom they are nurturing. Some of them will obviously remain with the ministry or organization for many years to come, and they may even become part of its leadership team at some point. When that happens they will bring with them a fresh perspective that the team needs to keep it from stagnating, and their incorporation will also provide for the team's vision to expand and to continue on long after the original team members are gone. Most leaders, as they grow older, traditionally think in terms of "passing the baton" to another, younger leader. Instead, why not encourage the generations to walk side-by-side as a leadership team that will continue to move forward as the vision expands?

But there may also be those that are nurtured whom God places there but for a season in order to receive an impartation that can only be offered by that particular leadership team. He will then move them elsewhere, and when He does they should be freely released and commissioned to that new calling with the full blessing of the leadership team. I remember feeling disappointed when one young couple left our church and started attending another. A year or so later, however, the husband came to see me and told me how much he appreciated everything that I had poured into his life while he was a part of our church. He went on to say that he had been able, in turn, to share much of what he had received from me with others at the church where he was now a member. Only then did I begin to see that the time spent with him was not wasted. It bore good fruit in a field other than my own, one to which I had no direct access.

THE HIGHER STANDARD

Obviously, I believe that the peer-level team is the best way to go. I believe it to be the higher standard which must be pursued if we are to achieve excellence in team leadership. This chapter simply presents an overview of what I see as some of the key benefits of having this kind of leadership team. If you are intrigued by this concept, please read on!

Chapter 4
Counting the Cost

When I was in my pre-teens, I decided that I wanted a .22 rifle. My parents, believing that I was now old enough and responsible enough, agreed that I could have one but that I would have to earn the money and pay for it myself. I, of course, felt this was extremely unfair since they had previously bought me lots of nice things, but they were resolute, so I began to plan how I could come up with the money. The first thing I realized was that using my allowance to buy it would not be a good idea for two reasons: first, if I saved it all toward the rifle, I would not have any money left for anything else; and second, based on the amount I received each week, it would take me a LONG time to save up enough to buy the rifle. That only left me with one other option (since I was too young and honest to rob a bank), I would have to think of some way to earn the money; I would have to work for it! Thus, I began my less-than-illustrious career of going door-to-door selling subscriptions to Grit magazine (which I recently discovered is still in print). I quickly learned that I was not cut out to be a salesman, but enough people took pity on me and bought subscriptions that I was ultimately able to earn enough money to buy the rifle. That rifle quickly became my most prized possession, and I took better care of it than anything else I owned. Why? Because I had to work hard to earn it; I made a personal investment (doing something I didn't really enjoy doing) in order to obtain something I considered worthy of the sacrifice required of me to acquire it.

Something worth having comes at a cost. King David understood this principle and demonstrated it when Ornan offered to give David his threshing floor which was located where God told David to build an altar. David's response recorded in 1Chron.21:24 (NASB) was, "I will not take what is yours for the Lord, or offer a burnt offering which costs me nothing," so he bought the field from Ornan. The same principle is true for having a peer-level team. It is not only well worth having, but it is also something that should bring glory to the Lord; therefore, it will cost something. These are some of the areas that will cost something.

DYING TO SELF

First and foremost, in order for a peer-level team to function properly, each member of the team must be willing to die to self. This means that each member of the team, when he becomes a part of that team, must lay down any personal agendas that he may be carrying. The team relationship is not intended to be a platform for the exhibition and promotion of each member's ministry. Instead, it is a place where the gifts and talents of each individual are blended together for the sake of the ministry which the team leads and oversees.

When I was the pastor of a church in a large metropolitan area, I would occasionally get a call from someone who was a recent graduate of a nearby Bible school asking if I might have an opening on my staff for a worship leader, a youth leader, or whatever it was that person felt called by God to be. Since the church was relatively small, my staff was made up entirely of volunteers. However, I always responded with an invitation to that person to come and be a part of our church, to embrace the vision of the church, and to begin to serve as a volunteer in that area of ministry. I explained that this would require that person to get a job outside the church initially, but I also told them that the position could possibly become a paid one in the future. No one ever took me up on my offer. Apparently, they were all looking for a position that would serve as a platform to help them fulfill their own personal agendas, one which would require very little sacrifice on their part.

The team relationship is not intended to be a place where one member uses that relationship, or any of the other team members, or the favor he accesses by being a part of that team as a means for personal gain. The relationship is not about furthering the selfish goals of the individuals on the team, and it is not about any one member receiving personal recognition above the others; it is about the team, as a whole, accomplishing the purpose for which the Lord brought it together --- to lead others in such a way as to help them become the people God intends them to be and to help them accomplish everything that He has planned for them in His Kingdom here on this earth. This is the essence of what it means to die to self when it comes to a peer-level team relationship.

And the greatest responsibility for being willing to die to self falls upon the recognized leader of the team. But dying to self is not an easy thing for the leader to do. Why? Because he was most likely the one who was initially given the vision for the ministry that the team leads, and it will be very difficult for him to avoid taking ownership of the vision in such a way that it becomes a personal agenda for him. He must constantly remember that the vision does not belong to him. It belongs to the Lord, and it has simply been entrusted to him as a stewardship. Yet, if he is willing to set the example of dying to self, even regarding the vision itself, it will be much easier for the other team members to do so, also.

SUBMISSION OF VISION

Speaking of vision, in order for the team to be able to accomplish everything that the Lord has planned for it, each member of the team must submit his own personal vision/visions to the corporate vision of the team. Now I am not saying that personal visions must be abandoned; I am saying that they must be submitted. This means that each member must consider how his personal vision can help fulfill the vision of the team as a whole rather than trying to use the team relationship as an opportunity to advance his own vision.

In my personal experience, I discovered that the visions God has given me have been fulfilled to a much higher level by submitting them to a larger corporate vision. What I saw accomplished in my ministry before becoming a part of the ICLC team pales in comparison to what I have seen accomplished since then! The vision of ICLC gave me a place where my own visions became a significant part of helping fulfill that larger one and where they, in turn, found greater expression and effectiveness than ever before.

The submission of personal visions to the corporate vision is something that every member of the team must do, even the leader of the team. And again, this is especially difficult for strong leaders because they are, by nature, visionaries. Vision is what motivates them, what keeps them going when others have already given up, and what gives them purpose in their lives. To be willing to submit their visions to a corporate vision is truly a sacrifice, but if the team is to function properly, it is something that they must also be willing to do.

OPENNESS AND HONESTY

There is also a price to be paid in the area of openness and honesty. When I was growing up, and especially when I was in college, I was pretty much an open book --- what you saw was basically the real me. However, as I entered into full-time ministry, that began to change; what you saw was not necessarily the real me. I began to adopt the persona of what I thought a pastor should be like instead of just being me. This happened for two main reasons: first, the generation of ministers who came before me and mentored me in the ways of ministry encouraged me to be careful about being too transparent with others because that would reveal too many of my personal weaknesses. They believed that the congregation would lose confidence in me if I did so, therefore, it was better if I did not let any of them get too close to me lest they see me for who I really was. That way I could maintain the image that they believed was what the congregation needed to see in order to properly respect me.

The second reason that I began to adopt this fake persona was that, deep down, I believed that the real me wasn't what a pastor should be like, so I often put on masks that represented what I thought a pastor should be, and I wore them before others instead of letting them see the real me. I finally discovered that truth is always the best approach to everything, and I began to just be me again. Seeing me for who I really am, warts and all, is actually more helpful for the people to whom I minister than seeing an image of someone who "has it all together." Seeing my humanity not only makes them realize that I really can relate to what they are going through, but it also shows them that if God can use me, He can surely use them, too! In Phil1:9-10 (NASB) Paul writes, "And this I pray, that your love may abound still more and more in real knowledge and all discernment, so that you may approve the things that are excellent, in order to be sincere and blameless until the day of Christ." The Greek word that is translated here as sincere (and translated as pure in many other versions) is *eilikrines* which, according to teknia.com, means "that which being viewed in the sunshine is found clear and pure." In classical Greek the same word was used to describe a sculpture as being "without wax." This meant that if the sculptor had used wax to cover any flaws in his creation, the light and heat of the sun would expose them. So what I am saying is that the only way to be truly open and honest is to take off the masks and to let others see us as we really are. We are to be real with each other --- sincere, without wax!

      Obviously, this does not mean that we go around blurting out everything that comes into our minds, or that we act upon every impulse that we feel. What I have discovered is that we, as Christians, are kind of like having three people live inside of us at the same time. We are the person God originally created us to be, we are the old (carnal) man that keeps trying to re-assert dominance in our lives, and we are the new creature that He is making us into after being born again. The real you is the person God created you to be. You are unique. God put you together in such a way as to create someone who will fit perfectly into the plans that He has for your life. No one else can be you. Your height, your build, your hair color, your ethnicity, your gender, your talents, your original personality, everything about you is a gift from God. As the Psalmist says in Ps.139:14 (NLT), "I praise you because I am fearfully and wonderfully made; your works are wonderful, I know that full well." How you express that real you is determined by how much you yield the original you to the new creature God wants you to be or to the old man that the devil wants you to keep falling back into, and there is a big difference between the two! The old man is the devil's attempt to corrupt and change the original you into someone who never reaches his full potential and who never fulfills his/her destiny in God. The new creature is God's work of building upon and enhancing the original you to the point that you reach your greatest potential as a person and are enabled to be the most effective you can be for His Kingdom here on this earth. Being open and honest means freely expressing the original you that is being transformed into the new creature that God is making you to be and then seeking help in the areas where the old man raises up his ugly head on a regular basis.

This is difficult for many of us to do because of personal insecurities and the fear of rejection. However, it is absolutely essential that we learn to do so, primarily for our own well-being. But we must also do so for the sake of the peer-level team to which we belong so that the team can function properly. If everyone on the team is open and honest in this way, then each member of the team is accepted for who he is, and he finds a place of security and freedom to grow more into the new creature that God is making him to be.

BEING PROPERLY CONFRONTATIONAL

Another price that must be paid is in the area of confrontations. A peer-level team must allow for confrontations to occur, but these confrontations must be handled properly. Most teams will have some members who are on one of the two extreme sides of the confrontation coin: those who seem to enjoy confrontations and those who don't want to "make waves." Both extremes are potentially destructive. Those who are more confrontational should be challenged to deal only with truly significant issues, and those who are non-confrontational should be encouraged to speak up.

If someone genuinely needs to be confronted because of ongoing sin areas in his life, it should be handled according to the principles laid out in Mt.18:15-17 (NIV). According to the instructions Jesus gives us there, that person should first be confronted privately by someone on the team. Should he refuse to listen to the one who first confronts him, he should then be approached again by the person who went to him the first time, but this time accompanied by one or two others from the team. He needs to understand that the issue being addressed is not just a matter of one person's opinion; it is something that is also recognized by others. In this application the team as a whole would take on the role of the church with the party being brought before the team as a whole should he still refuse to repent and seek help. Only as a last resort should he be removed from the team. In most cases, the first or second level of confrontation will resolve the issue.

But there will also be disagreements and differences of opinion regarding issues that the team as a whole addresses. Open discussion over these issues should be allowed and encouraged so that those issues can be fully examined before important decisions are made. Many years ago, I was in a team meeting where one of the key leaders of the team announced that everyone on the team was going to be required to do a certain thing. It's been so long now that I don't remember what it was that was being required. But what I do remember is that I politely (I think) challenged what was being imposed upon us because we had not been given the opportunity to discuss it before the decision was made. This same man, then, while looking directly at me, sternly informed all of us that the decision had been made by the recognized primary leader of the team and that we were not to challenge it. While his intimidating response silenced us from voicing any disagreement, it undermined what we were trying to build upon as a peer-level team. In fact, it was not until after this man was eventually removed from the team due to numerous unresolved issues in his life that the intimidation factor was broken and a more open relationship restored within the team.

What must be true in all confrontations, whether they be on a personal level or on the team level, is that everyone involved has to maintain a humble heart. And those doing the confronting must do so only because they truly want to see people helped and because they sincerely desire to make sure that the decisions made by the team are pleasing to God. Without confrontation, no one changes on the personal level, and mistakes are made on the corporate level. However, when there is misuse through constant confrontation, people begin to feel demeaned on the personal level, and nothing significant is accomplished on the team level. Confrontations must be allowed, but they must be done properly.

GIVING PROPER PROTECTION

Every member of the team must know that he will be "protected" by the other members of that team. In a peer-level team where openness and honesty are encouraged and practiced, one person's areas of weakness are going to be exposed to others on the team --- sometimes through confrontations, sometimes simply because of the close relationships that are engendered, and sometimes because a team member asks for help. Each member of the team must feel confident that no one else on the team will expose his weaknesses outside of the team setting. He must feel confident that he will be protected by the others on the team as he makes himself vulnerable by being open and transparent. Prov.17:9 (NIV) says, "Whoever would foster love covers over an offense, but whoever repeats the matter separates close friends."

I heard about a man who shared with his pastor a struggle that he was having in his marriage. The pastor expressed concern, gave him some suggestions on how to handle the problem, and then prayed for him.

The man left feeling much better, but a few days later he discovered that others in the church knew about certain details of his marital problems that he had shared only with the pastor. He and his wife felt so betrayed by this that they left that church without receiving the help they needed in their marriage. Thereafter, he refused to attend church anywhere, and he and his wife eventually divorced. His lingering bitterness from that experience made it impossible for him to receive help from anyone because he had given up on believing that he could ever again trust those in authority, spiritual or otherwise.

This kind of thing should never happen on a peer-level team. However, it does not mean that the team should engage in cover-ups. It must be understood by everyone on the team that if something must be made public or reported to the proper authorities, excuses will not be made for that person, and those kinds of things will not be kept secret. For example, if a team member becomes involved in criminal activities, he should be reported to the proper authorities. Or if, after being confronted properly, a team member is unwilling to repent of attitudes or actions that could greatly harm himself or others (whether team members or not), or if he refuses to address areas in his life that go contrary to the purposes of God for that ministry, he should be publicly removed from the team.

At the same time, each team member must be assured that those areas of weakness in his life that are not dangerous or destructive to others, those that do not negatively affect the purposes of God, and even those more serious issues in his life that are in the process of being dealt with properly, will all remain confidential. "Protecting" each other means that discretion and confidentiality will be practiced by all. It means that, with only rare exceptions, what happens in the team setting will stay in the team setting.

A SERVANT'S HEART

And finally, in order for a peer-level team to function properly, every member must cultivate a servant's heart. I once heard a servant's heart defined as getting excited about making others successful. Every member of the team should be excited about helping the other team members become that which God wants them to be, and he should be enthusiastic about helping all of them accomplish everything that God has planned for them in this life. This means that he must, from the heart, put their success and fulfillment, both in life and in ministry, before his own. Romans 12:10 (NASB) tells us, "Be devoted to one another in brotherly love; give preference to one another in honor." Since this is not something that comes easily for most of us, it requires a deeper level of dying to self. This is what Jesus was talking about in Mt.20:25-28 (NIV) where He said, "You know that the rulers of the Gentiles lord it over them, and their high officials exercise authority over them. Not so with you. Instead, whoever wants to become great among you must be your servant, and whoever wants to be first must be your slave --- just as the Son of Man did not come to be served, but to serve, and to give his life as a ransom for many."

But the encouraging irony of having a servant's heart is that while we are busy helping others reach their potential, God is at work making sure that we are not passed over. For example, after spending many years serving the prophet Elijah, Elisha received a double portion of the anointing that Elijah had carried. Jesus addressed this principle in Mt.23:11-12 (NIV) where He said, "The greatest among you will be your servant. For those who exalt themselves will be humbled, and those who humble themselves will be exalted."

The beauty is that when a servant's heart is present in all of the members of a leadership team, not only do the individuals on that team benefit, but the team as a whole becomes more effective in accomplishing the purposes that God has for it in His Kingdom.

IT IS WORTH IT!

There is an expression in Spanish that I like very much, "vale la pena." It is regularly translated, "It's worth it." The literal translation, however, is more like, "It is worth the pain, the heartache, the trouble, the labor." It is something a mother would say when she first gets to hold her newborn child, or what a medical school graduate would say upon receiving his diploma and finishing his internship, or what an Olympic gold medal winner would say after all the years of sacrifice to become the best in his field. Yes, a price must be paid to have an effectively functioning peer-level team, but as will be seen in the following chapters, "vale la pena!"

Chapter 5
Making it Work

In order for a peer-level team to function properly, esprit de corps is absolutely essential, and it is the primary key to "making it work" and to keeping it working. Webster's dictionary defines esprit de corps as "the common spirit existing in the members of a group and inspiring enthusiasm, devotion, and strong regard for the honor of the group." Even though it is usually present to some degree in the formative stages of a peer-level team, it is imperative that it be continually developed and improved upon; it is not something that should be taken for granted as the years roll by. As most of us have learned, a marriage relationship is something that requires constant input in order for it to remain vibrant over the years. So, also, a peer-level team requires constant reinforcement in order to maintain a healthy esprit de corps, especially as some of the members of the team come and go for various reasons. This chapter is focused on some of the most important things that help promote esprit de corps on the team.

COMUNICATION

The first key to developing and maintaining esprit de corps is communication. Even as personal relationships suffer and often fail for lack of healthy, ongoing communication, those relationships also become stronger when communication is encouraged and engaged in consistently. The same is true for the team relationship. Communication is essential!

In the team setting, the foundational thing that must be regularly communicated is the team's vision. The members of a peer-level team are there mainly because of the vision that it pursues. In reality, the vision is even more important to them than the team leader's personality, popularity, or individual charisma. However, it is the team leader who should be the standard-bearer of that vision, and he should regularly rehearse it (or some aspect of it) to the other members of the team, thereby fanning the flame in all of them. When this is done regularly each member will, in turn, be inspired to continue doing his part to see that vision fulfilled, and he will encourage the others on the team to do the same. This is especially important during those "winter" seasons when nothing (or very little) outwardly appears to be happening in seeing the vision accomplished. I feel certain that there were many times during those forty years spent walking around in the wilderness waiting for an unbelieving generation to die off that Joshua and Caleb repeatedly encouraged each other to keep believing and not lose heart. The vision that God had given Moses regarding the land that He promised to Israel had, in turn, been imparted to both of them by Moses. And I believe that they kept it alive by recounting to each other everything they had witnessed when they had spied out the land. Likewise, the vision of the team that has been imparted to the members by their leader must be kept alive by sharing it regularly with each other!

Obviously, another necessary part of communication is the sharing of information and not just information regarding the time and place of the next meeting. Each member of the team should also be aware of the significant things that are happening which are relevant to the team as a whole or to individual members of the team. For example, if the ministry is in a financial bind, everyone on the team should know about it. Or if one member is sick or struggling in some personal area, the others should know so they can pray for him and try to help him through it. And on the positive side, if something good happens for the team or for someone on the team, everyone should hear about it as quickly as possible so that they can all rejoice together. When information is not properly and consistently shared in a timely manner, problems are sure to arise. What would happen if a member of the team were constantly finding out about things after the fact (even though it be unintentional)? He would probably begin to wonder if he were really needed or even wanted on the team. If this were to go uncorrected, he may then begin to pull back from participating fully with the team, and the team would lose the benefit of his gifts and talents; or, worse case scenario, he may eventually become disillusioned and (intentionally or unintentionally) begin to sow discord among others on the team or with people outside the team. Communicating information may seem to be a small thing, but Song of Solomon 2:15 (NIV) tells us that it is "the little foxes that ruin the vineyards."

The other significant aspect of communication is sharing our hearts with one another. If we are to have an effective peer-level team, we must know each other well enough that we know what burns within each of us, what motivates us, what our dreams are, and even what frightens us. In a marriage this sharing of the heart is one of the main things that a wife wants from her husband. Without it she feels like she is on the outside looking in. In a team relationship this is one of the keys to being a true peer-level team. Opening our hearts to one another requires trust, and trust is something that must be established through the proving of the relationships over a period of time. I heard a story about a tightrope walker who drew a crowd when he stretched a cable across Niagara Falls and began walking back and forth using a long balancing pole. When the crowd grew large enough, he abandoned the pole and, much to the astonishment of the crowd, he pushed a wheelbarrow across and back. Upon his return, and after the cheering subsided, he asked who believed he could do it again. Of course everyone, having seen him do it once, said they believed he could. There was a different response entirely, however, when he then asked for a volunteer to ride in the wheelbarrow as he pushed it across one more time! Openness in sharing our hearts with each other is based on trust and should not be demanded in the early stages of building the team, but it is something that should be pursued and developed as the relationships deepen and as trust is established and confirmed.

SPIRIT OF AGREEMENT

I have yet to meet someone who is always in total agreement with me. In fact, I have never heard of any two people who are regularly in complete agreement on everything, and I am quite certain they are nowhere to be found. The truth is that we are all different; we see things differently, we think about things differently, and we have different tastes and preferences. This is one of the things that makes life interesting, and it is something that makes a team more effective. So then, is it possible for there to be total agreement in a peer-level team? No, it is not.

That is why there must be a spirit of agreement. When it comes to decisions the team makes that will affect the ministry it leads, every attempt should be made for everyone on the team to be in agreement. But occasionally that is not possible. In such cases the persons who are not in agreement must be willing to support the decision that is made, and they should do so in a spirit of agreement. What this means is that when they are asked about that decision by people who are not a part of team, their response must always be supportive of that decision. For example, they should never say "they decided" or even "the team decided," but they should say instead, "we decided." And the way they make that statement must convey their support for the decision even though they were not in agreement with it. Therefore, before leaving the meeting where the decision is made, they must make sure that their hearts are right regarding supporting the decision; otherwise their disagreement will be conveyed in spite of the words they choose to use. [Please note that I will address how to handle team disagreements in more detail in later chapters. If they are handled properly, there should be no problem walking in a spirit of agreement.] A spirit of agreement, then, is very important to maintaining esprit de corps because when everyone walks in a spirit of agreement, no one worries about anything being said outside of the team setting that could undermine the team.

DIVERSITY IN UNITY

As I stated above, we are all different. In a peer-level team this is not only a good thing, it is a necessary thing. If all the members of the team were just alike, the team would not be very effective. Even though everyone on the team would share the same strengths, they would also share the same weaknesses, and those weaknesses would be magnified and multiplied to the detriment of the organization that the team oversees. Yet it is surprising how many leadership teams are made up of individuals who are very much like each other. This usually happens because the team leader feels more secure and less threatened by people who have gifts, talents, and personalities that are similar to his own, so these are the kind of people he initially chooses for his team, and the pattern tends to continue.

The ICLC team of which I am a member is made up of some of the most diverse individuals I have ever been around. There are some who are quiet and thoughtful, some who speak spontaneously, some who like to kid and joke around, some who are more somber, some who tend toward mysticism (in a good way), and some who are very practical in their approach to things. We also have all five ministry gifts as listed in Eph.4:11 (apostles, prophets, evangelists, pastors, and teachers) represented on the team. In spite of all this diversity, we have the kind of relationship (mutual respect and appreciation) that allows us to work well together --- even the teachers and the evangelists get along with each other!

The Apostle Paul addresses this principle of diversity in unity in great detail in 1Cor.12:14-21 (NIV) where he writes, "Even so the body is not made up of one part but of many. Now if the foot should say, 'Because I am not a hand, I do not belong to the body,' it would not for that reason stop being part of the body. And if the ear should say, 'Because I am not an eye, I do not belong to the body,' it would not for that reason stop being part of the body. If the whole body were an eye, where would the sense of hearing be? If the whole body were an ear, where would the sense of smell be? But in fact God has placed the parts in the body, every one of them, just as he wanted them to be. If they were all one part, where would the body be? As it is, there are many parts, but one body. The eye cannot say to the hand, 'I don't need you!' And the head cannot say to the feet, 'I don't need you!'"

Even as the human body is made up of distinctly different individual parts that all contribute to the proper functioning of the body, so also should be the makeup of a peer-level team. A variety of different gifts, talents, and personality types are necessary for the team to function properly.

GENUINE APPRECIATION

But simply recognizing the need for diversity and incorporating it into the team is not enough by itself. Each member (especially the leader of the team) must also appreciate and value the differences in every other member. According to the principles that Paul expressed in the scripture passage above, one member should never compare himself to another member of the team and conclude that because he is not like that one he is either inferior or superior to that person. No one is inferior or superior to the others, he is just different, and those differences are something that the team needs! When each team member embraces this truth and truly values the others on the team for both their similarities and their differences, he is then able to appreciate and to draw upon the strengths that the others possess.

But feeling appreciation for the others is only the first step. That appreciation must also be verbalized and demonstrated. Verbalizing it can be done by simply saying something like "Brother, I appreciate how you handled that," or "I appreciate how faithful you have been to the team," or

"Thank you for your input today; it really encouraged me." These kinds of statements confirm to the others that they are valuable parts of the team.

And when these statements are then followed up by actions that demonstrate that they are valued, they find themselves becoming more and more solidly anchored in the team. For example, when I invite other team members (or anyone else, for that matter) to accompany me on one of my ministry trips, I try to make it a point to convey to them that I want them with me because the gifts and anointing that they carry will add a dynamic to our ministry together that will greatly bless those to whom we minister. I make sure that they are given as many opportunities as possible to share what they have been given. This helps me demonstrate, in a very practical way, how much I value them.

Genuine appreciation for each other promotes esprit de corps because it shows each member of the team, regardless of his own individual differences, that he is truly valued and accepted by the others on the team. This makes him feel more complete as a person and more effective in his area of ministry. And it gives him a greater sense of value and belonging.

COMMUNION

The team that prays, shares, and plays together, stays together! Fellowship in the three areas of spirit (prays), soul (shares), and body (plays) are what communion is all about. It's about friendship, and friendships are developed by spending time doing the kinds of things together that knit us more closely to each other in spirit, soul, and body. Many times, the primary interactions that team members have with each other are on the soul level; they discuss such things as pressings issues, future plans, and vision during team meetings, but the other two areas are often neglected. One of the things I appreciate about the team meetings we have with ICLC is that, in addition to soul-sharing, we also spend time praying together and waiting on the Lord, then we share with each other what we believe God is giving us. We also take time to pray for each other. This fellowship on the spirit level helps draw us even closer to each other. In fact, it is the primary ingredient in the glue that binds us together.

But because most of us live in different parts of the country and because our semi-annual meetings are necessarily devoted almost entirely to spirit and soul issues, there is not much time for fellowship on the physical/activities level. One thing that I like to do to help satisfy the need for fellowship in this area is to invite other team members to accompany me when I travel to other nations to minister. This way, in addition to having ample time to share together on the spirit and soul levels by ministering together and visiting over meals and such, I also try to plan times for some shared activities. For example, on one of my trips to minister in a conference in Acapulco, I invited two other members of our team to accompany me. I made sure we all arrived two days before the conference began so that we would have a day to charter a boat for deep-sea fishing together. We had a great time catching lots of tuna and team-catching two large marlins (sail fish)! We became closer friends and developed a stronger bond because of fellowshipping on all three levels on that trip. Spirit, soul, and body fellowship among team members promote esprit de corps. Remember, a team that prays, shares, and plays together, stays together!

ENCOURAGEMENT

I do not know of anyone who never needs encouragement. Something about our makeup as humans causes us to need and feed on encouragement; those who receive it regularly seem to be happier and more productive, and those who receive very little of it seem to struggle in many areas of their lives. The Bible speaks a lot about encouragement, and obviously Paul understood its importance because he wrote in 1Thes.5:11-14 (NAS), "Therefore encourage one another and build up one another, just as you also are doing. But we request of you, brethren, that you appreciate those who diligently labor among you, and have charge over you in the Lord and give you instruction, and that you esteem them very highly in love because of their work. Live in peace with one another. We urge you, brethren, admonish the unruly, encourage the fainthearted, help the weak, be patient with everyone."

What I find interesting in this passage is that Paul alludes to three of the main expressions of true encouragement. First, encouragement is giving someone praise for everything that merits it. Please understand that praise is not flattery. Flattery generally focuses *to excess* on a person's accomplishments or on things over which that person has no control (such as natural beauty or a God-given talent of some sort), and the key problem with flattery is that it is insincere. An overabundance of flattery tends to engender pride in the recipient, and the flatterer is usually only doing it for selfish reasons. Praise, on the other hand, is an acknowledgement of someone's personal accomplishments and is accompanied by written or verbal expressions of recognition to that person regarding those accomplishments. Sincere praise coming from someone who understands the investments and sacrifices made by that person in order to attain that accomplishment is very encouraging to the recipient. It makes him or her desire to continue pursuing excellence. When team members properly praise one another as it is warranted, they build each other up; and they demonstrate that they esteem/value one another.

Another way of encouraging others is by expressing and demonstrating appreciation for them. One divisive strategy the devil uses against teams is to make one of its members feel unappreciated or under-appreciated. If that person invests heavily in trying to do his part in helping the team fulfill its vision, yet no one seems to notice, he often falls prey to discouragement and feelings of isolation which then usually cause that person to pull back from his involvement with the team in some way. He may even eventually leave the team altogether. The easiest way to express appreciation is with a simple, "Thank you for …" and name something specific. This should become a habit that each team member develops and practices regularly with the others on the team. When this is accompanied by an occasional public expression of appreciation, everyone is encouraged to "keep on keeping on" and to become progressively better at carrying out his role on the team.

The third significant way that we can encourage others is by challenging them to strive for excellence in everything they do and by helping them overcome their areas of weakness. When I am struggling with my ability to accomplish something important, and I am beginning to feel discouraged, there is a positive change in my attitude when someone close to me says, "Come on, man, you've got this!" That simple word of encouragement becomes a challenge that builds confidence; it make me believe that I can do it, and I try even harder than before. When that person also says to me, "I've got your back," I know that he is aware of my areas of weakness and that he will take up the slack for me in those areas. This is what happened when Aaron and Hur held up Moses' hands so that Joshua and the army of Israel could defeat the Amalekites (Exodus 17). The rod that Moses was lifting up was the key to victory, but he was too weak in himself to hold it up long enough for that victory to be won; he needed the help of others. We need to be there for each other during those times when we are needed the most. I believe this is what Paul had in mind when he said in the passage above, "encourage the fainthearted, help the weak, be patient with everyone."

A number of years ago the church where I was the pastor went through a crisis which deeply affected both the church and me personally. In the midst of this, another pastor and close friend contacted me and offered to help in any way he could; then he said something that surprised and encouraged me greatly. He said, "Whatever I have in the bank is yours if you need it." We were able to come through the problem without needing the money, but his sincere offer meant the world to me. It helped encourage me to keep going when I wanted to give up.

Esprit de corps. It is an essential ingredient for an effective peer-level team, and it is developed and kept alive through communication, a spirit of agreement, diversity in unity, genuine appreciation for each other, communion, and encouragement. It is essential to "making it work" for a peer-level team.

Chapter 6
Before You Say "I Do"

It is always a good idea for two people who want to get married to receive counseling beforehand. Why? Because they need someone to try to help them understand that marriage is much more than just romantic feelings. In order for the marriage to last, there are certain commitments that they should make to each other and that they should be able to expect from each other.

It must also be understood by all members of a peer-level team that there are certain things that they should expect to give to each other and to receive from each other in order for the team to be successful. When each member commits himself to do his best to live up to these expectations, everyone on the team will feel more secure in the team relationship as a whole and also in the personal relationships between team members.

EXPECT TO BE VALUED

First, it should be expected that the team members will genuinely value each other --- not just for what each one brings to the team setting with his own personal gifts and talents but also for who he is as a person. Because of my own insecurities I used to feel uncomfortable around (perhaps even threatened by) people who saw things differently than I did and who freely expressed themselves accordingly. As a result, I tended to hold them at arm's length, and I was unwilling to look past our differences or to make any attempt to see them for who they really were. But over the years I have come to see these people in a different light; now I try to look past our differences and get to know them personally. Consequently, I have found that their disagreement does not necessarily mean that they are against me, but they simply see things from a different perspective. I have learned that I need their input to help me better evaluate things. I not only value them for their input, but many of them even become good friends. When I was part of a church youth group back in the early 60's, we used to sing a chorus that stated that no man is an island and that no man stands alone; that we should to embrace each man's joy and each man's grief as our own. It encouraged us to understand that we need each another and to defend each man as our brother and as our friend. Obviously, we cannot feel this way about everyone in the whole world, but it should definitely be how we value each member of the team.

EXPECT TO USE YOUR STRENGTHS

Each member of the team should also expect to be allowed and encouraged to work in the areas of his greatest strengths. For example, if I were asked to head up a door-to-door evangelism program, I could do it, but I would not do it very well because that is not an area where I am particularly gifted. But ask me to preach or teach or lead a small group, and I am definitely in my element. In a peer-level leadership team each of the members is a leader in his own right, or he would not be there. But it must be understood that his leadership anointing is greatest in the areas of his strongest gifts and talents, and to ask him to be responsible to give oversight to areas where he is not gifted will have undesirable consequences. He will grow frustrated, those he oversees will become frustrated, and the ministry in that area will suffer.

Now I realize that others may recognize potential strengths in us that we have not yet seen in ourselves, and that those areas should be developed by challenging us to experience new things. Usually, the best way to help us develop them is to put us with someone who is already strong in those areas instead of throwing us into the deep end of the pool by giving us a responsibility for which we are not prepared, and then hoping we quickly learn how to swim.

EXPECT YOUR WEAKNESSES TO BE STRENGTHENED

It should also be expected that we will always try to strengthen each other's weaknesses. As we begin to open our hearts and lives to each other, and thus make ourselves vulnerable to each other, our areas of weakness are going to be exposed. Not only should we "cover" each other (as I mentioned earlier) and take up the slack for one another, but we should also try to help each other overcome those weaknesses. Obviously, I am not talking here about personality differences and insignificant personal idiosyncrasies that do not affect our team involvement and that do not damage the team's effectiveness. But if an exposed weakness in a team member is potentially harmful to the team or to others, that person should be addressed regarding that weakness in a spirit of love and humility. Then, help should be offered to him.

I know of a team leader who had a real problem with arrogance which became obvious, not only to the other team members, but also to people outside the team context. And even though it became evident that his arrogance was casting shadows on his personal ministry and damaging the testimony of the team as a whole, the other members of the team were reluctant to address the issue with him. Instead, possibly because of being intimidated by his strong personality and because they recognized that his areas of strength were a tremendous blessing to the team, they chose to make excuses for his behavior instead of confronting him about this weakness. As a result, things only got worse. Sadly, when he was finally confronted, he did not respond well, and he removed himself from the team. But by that time, many people had been deeply wounded by the way he treated them, and as a consequence, the reputation of the whole team suffered for many years after.

So then, we should not only be willing to help strengthen the weaknesses of others on the team, but when our own weaknesses are exposed we should also be willing to humble ourselves and receive the help that is offered to us. And even though it may be painful for us,

Prov.27:6 (NASB) tells us that the wounds of a friend are faithful. This is the kind of friend who sticks closer than a brother (Prov.18:24, NIV). We should be like the wise men of Prov.9:8 (NIV) who love those who reprove them. The team will grow stronger when we care enough to try to strengthen each other's weaknesses.

EXPECT MUTUAL LOVING SUBMISSION

Receiving help requires that we be willing to follow Paul's directive in Ephesians 5:21 (NIV), "Submit to one another out of reverence for Christ." Every member of a peer-level team must be willing to submit (present for examination, evaluation, etc.) his life to the other team members. To do this wholeheartedly and completely is not something that most people will do in the early stages of their relationship with the team, nor should it be demanded of them at this point. However, as the relationship deepens and trust is established, submission should be both expected and given by everyone on the team.

Actually, this is not such a difficult thing to do if the other part of this expectation is followed --- that we love one another. In fact, love is not an option. In John 15:12 (NASB) Jesus commanded us to love one another in the same way that He loves us. This means that we choose to demonstrate "agape" love to each other by desiring God's best for each other and by doing everything we can to help make that happen. This means that we are willing to lay down our lives for each other (Jn,15:13). Yes, willing to die if necessary, but more than that, we must be willing to put each other's needs before our own. If we all seek to apply 1Cor.13 to our team relationships, we will satisfy this expectation, and it will be easy to submit to each other.

EXPECT THE BEST FROM EACH OTHER

It should also be expected that each member of the team will give the best that he has to offer in everything that he does with and for the team. This is one of the main ways that a person's commitment to the team is expressed. For example, a rookie who is trying to earn a place on an NFL team's roster will obviously do everything he can to demonstrate his best qualities to the coaches; he will give his best. But this should also be true for the returning veterans on the team. They should not only desire to remain a part of the team, but they should also want to do the best they can to try to help the team go all the way to the Super Bowl. So, too, each member of a peer-level team should give his best so that the team can accomplish everything that God has planned for it.

Now, a team member's commitment to the team should never come before his personal relationship with the Lord and only rarely before his commitments to his own family, but apart from that he, should be willing to make whatever sacrifices are necessary in order to fulfill his responsibilities to the team to the very best of his abilities. Recently, I heard about an NFL player who quit giving his best to his team because he had been secretly approached by another team and told that they would pick him up and pay him more if he could manage to get released by the team he was currently on. He did just that, and as a result, his team did release him, and the other team picked him up. Obviously, his commitment was only to himself; it was never to his team. Team members must feel an obligation of commitment to the team. And when they do, they will have no problem giving their best.

EXPECT INTEGRITY

Integrity is something that should be expected from every team member. Wikipedia.com defines integrity as "a personal choice, an uncompromising and predictably consistent commitment to honor moral, ethical, spiritual and artistic values and principles." In 1Tim.3 (NASB), Paul lists several qualifications for an overseer. Among them are that he must be "above reproach" (v.2) and that "he must have a good reputation with those outside" (v.7). A man of integrity will easily satisfy these requirements.

Integrity does not imply perfection, but rather the pursuit of it and the willingness to deal properly with failures. A good leader (and every member of a peer-level team is a leader in his own right) is always willing to admit his errors and ask for forgiveness. I believe that if Richard Nixon had admitted what he had done and asked for forgiveness, the American people would have stood by him instead of forcing him to resign. Sadly, the standard of integrity has been abandoned by much of the world today in favor of personal or corporate expediency. This must never be the case for any member of a peer-level team or for the team as a whole. The blessing of the Lord is upon people of integrity.

EXPECT TO LAY DOWN PERSONAL EXPECTATIONS

Nearly every time I receive a promise from the Lord, or when I am about to begin a new area of ministry, or when I prepare to minister somewhere new, the first thing I tend to do is imagine what it will be like when it happens. I am sure that this is common to most of us, and it is not a bad thing in itself. However, if the way I picture it becomes an expectation and anticipation of exactly how it will be, I am nearly always wrong! And if it is worse than I imagined, I am disappointed. And if I do not let go of the disappointment, I usually fail to embrace the fullness of God's plan for me there.

Imagination and anticipation are good as long as they remain very general. In fact, expectation is also a very good thing as long as it does not focus us on specific details. For example, I know that God has promised to meet all of my needs "according to the riches of His glory in Christ Jesus" (Phil.4:19, NIV). I have a daily expectation that I will see this promise fulfilled. However, if I begin to put my own interpretation onto exactly how that will happen, I will nearly always be wrong and disappointed when it doesn't happen that way. And in extreme cases, an expectation that is too specific can cause problems. Many years ago I knew a man who, even though he could have easily found a job that paid well, chose to be unemployed. When his wife told me what he was doing, I paid him a visit and asked him why he wasn't working. What he told me was that he knew God was going to take care of him by sending him a dog with a bag full of cash in its mouth! Well, needless to say, he eventually went back to work, but during the time that he was waiting, his family suffered because of his misplaced expectation. Now don't get me wrong, I know that God can give very specific and detailed promises. And when that happens, we should expect exactly what we have been told. However, if the specifics are born in our own imaginations, we should lay them down.

Now as for how all of this applies to a peer-level team, the members of the team must be careful to examine both the expectations that they carry with them upon joining the team, along with those expectations that will arise during the course of their involvement with the team. This applies to areas such as what they expect the team relationship to be like, how they expect to be utilized in their ministries, and what they expect the fulfillment of the team's goals will look like. They must always have expectations that God will do everything that He promises to do, but they must only be specific in their expectations when God is specific.

When every member of the team understands what is expected of him and does his best to fulfill these expectations, the team as a whole benefits, as does each person on the team.

Chapter 7
Follow the Leader

The recognized team leader is the key to having a really good peer-level team. He is the one who initially and ultimately determines whether or not the team will be truly peer-level. If he has the vision for it and is willing to do everything he can to make it work, then it can happen. However, seeing it come about will be a challenge for him. As a naturally strong leader, somewhere along the way he will probably have adopted some philosophies of leadership that may not fit well within a peer-level team relationship. He may also have developed some unfavorable character issues that will need to be addressed in order for the team to function properly. I encourage every team leader (or potential team leader) to honestly evaluate himself by what is in this chapter.

NOT DICTATORIAL

First, he must not be a dictator. In fact, he must not even consider himself to be the boss within the team context. If he does, he will never see the other members of the team as his peers. I believe that much of what is called leadership today is not the kind of leadership that God intended. I have addressed this in great detail in my book, *The Jefe Factor: Exposing the Jefe and Revealing the Leader in Each of Us*. A Jefe is someone who holds a leadership position but uses it for his own personal gain. A true leader, on the other hand, sees his position as an opportunity to help the organization he works for and the people he oversees to become the best they can possibly be. I recommend that every leader read this book, whether or not he is the leader of the team.

HUMBLE

The team leader should be humble. Humility means that he recognizes that he has been placed by God in the position that he occupies simply because it is part of God's plan for his life and part of his role in the Kingdom of God. He is not there because he is better than anyone else or because God loves him any more than He loves even an unsaved person. He is simply there because God chose to put him there. He should realize that God made him the way He did so that he can fulfill what he has been called to do in that position.

This understanding will then help him to be more approachable and more compassionate. Quite often, when I was a senior pastor, I received feedback that people felt uncomfortable trying to talk to me, and that they wondered if I genuinely cared about their problems. I didn't understand this because I regularly assured everyone that my door was always open, yet few actually took me up on the offer. That all changed, however, when God showed me the pride in my life (which I described in an earlier chapter) and helped me become a more humble person. I then understood that people had felt the way they did because I had, without realizing it, allowed my pride to cause me to become somewhat distant and less compassionate than I should have been when I was relating to others. It was not intentional on my part, but it was what I conveyed to those looking to me for ministry and leadership. The team leader must be humble in order to have a good relationship with the other members of the team.

One synonym for humility is meekness, which is often misinterpreted as weakness. Numbers 12:3 (KJV) describes Moses as being meek; in fact, more so than anyone else. But anyone who is familiar with the story of Moses knows that he was in no way a weak man. So, a better understanding of what it means to be meek can be found by looking at the Greek word "praeis" which is translated as the word meek in the New Testament. It describes someone who accepts, without disputing or resisting, the dealings of God in his life. One example of this is found in Mt.5:5 (NIV) which says, "Blessed are the meek, for they will inherit the earth." In classical Greek, it was the same word that was used to describe a horse that had been properly broken and trained. Meekness, then, describes a person whose own self-will has been broken to the point that he has submitted all of his strengths (spirit, soul, and body) to the will of the Lord. A leader who is humble/meek is not a weak individual; he is still (and should be) bold, confident, and decisive in his leadership role, but he does not use those strengths to dominate others or to force his own will upon them. Instead, he sees himself as first among equals --- neither superior nor inferior to them. He sees himself simply as their servant-leader.

INCLUSIVE

Speaking of being decisive, the team leader should avoid making unilateral decisions that affect the rest of the team or the ministry that the team oversees. For example, there was a pastor of a church of about 250 members who had a team of elders that he worked with in giving oversight to the church. One Sunday morning he announced from the pulpit that he was calling the church to a forty-day fast. Now he had prayed much about it, and he was convinced that this was what God wanted for the church, but the problem was that he had discussed none of this with the elders ahead of time. The first they heard about it was when he announced it to the church. Did the pastor have the authority to do this? Absolutely! However, was it wise of him to do so without involving the elders in his decision beforehand? Absolutely not! By making this unilateral decision, whether he meant to or not, he sent a message to the elders that they were nothing more than "yes men" and that he did not trust them or value their input on significant issues. A peer-level team is not truly peer-level unless everyone on the team is allowed to be involved in the decision-making process.

When the leader includes the rest of the team, he conveys to them that they are not simply his "yes" men, instead they are the people that he wants and needs by his side. And by involving them in the process, he often avoids making unwise and potentially costly decisions. Prov.12:15 (NASB) says it this way, "The way of a fool is right in his own eyes, but a wise man is he who listens to counsel."

SECURE

Next, the team leader must be someone who is secure in who he is as a person, secure in his personal gifts and talents, secure in his relationship with the Lord, and secure in his leadership position in God's kingdom here on earth. A synonym for secure is confident. To be effective in his role as team leader, he must be infused with confidence.

Part of Webster's online dictionary definition of secure is "not feeling suspicion or distrust." If the team leader is not secure in the key areas mentioned above, he will tend to interpret disagreement as rejection, input as correction, and new ideas as subversion. Insecurity in the team leader must be addressed and corrected; otherwise, he will begin to grow suspicious of the other team members' motives, and he will begin to misinterpret almost everything they say and do. He will also feel threatened by them if they should receive acclaim and recognition in their ministry to others. A classic example of this is King Saul who became jealous of David when songs were sung about David killing ten thousands of Israel's enemies compared to Saul killing only thousands. He then began to believe that David was trying to take the kingdom from him (1Sam.18:6-8). It was not long before Saul started looking for ways to get rid of David. A deep-seated insecurity in the team leader can be very destructive to a peer-level team.

A secure team leader, however, allows and encourages the other team members to express themselves freely, and he rejoices when they exercise their gifts and talents to minister in ways that he cannot. Because he is secure, he can do this without feeling threatened either personally or in his position as the team leader.

One example of a secure leader is the apostle Paul whose security in his calling is evident in how often he confidently referred to himself as an apostle. He wasn't boasting, just stating a fact. One such reference is in 1Cor.9:2 (NASB) where he writes, "If to others I am not an apostle, at least I am to you; for you are the seal of my apostleship in the Lord." The leader of the peer-level team MUST be someone who is secure in all the areas mentioned above.

NOT POSSESSIVE

Even though the team leader should be secure both personally and in his position with the team, he should always hold that position with an open hand. In other words, he should recognize that the position is his only as long as the Lord wants him to have it. If he ever closes his fist around, it he will no longer possess the position; instead, it will possess him. This means that he will then close himself off to the possibility that God may have something else for him to do at some point, and he will become so personally identified with his position that he will begin to jealously guard it, because that is where he finds his sense of value. If this should happen, then both he and the team (and probably the ministry they oversee as well) will begin to move toward becoming ineffective.

Now, God puts some team leaders in that positon until they die, while He chooses to use others in that position only long enough to fulfill certain objectives. When those objectives are accomplished, God will then desire to move them on to something else that He has planned for them, but only after raising up others to take that position. In either case, the team leader must never believe that he "owns" the position. Even the apostle Paul saw his ministry as a stewardship entrusted to him by God (see Col.1:25 NASB). So, too, the leader must see his position as a stewardship from the Lord.

RELEASING

When the leader is secure and understands that his position is a stewardship, it then becomes easier for him to trust the other members of the team to the degree that he willingly releases them. This means, first of all, that he encourages them to function with the authority and freedom they need in order to fulfill their responsibilities. He genuinely wants them to exercise their gifts and ministries with total confidence, both within the team setting and as representatives of the team when apart from it, and he trusts them to do so.

Next, he releases them to follow the leading of the Holy Spirit as they fulfill their callings. This means that they are free to minister according to their own gifts and talents instead of being expected to do things a certain way. A good team leader recognizes that the way others do things will probably be different than how he would do them (perhaps not even as well as he would do them), but he refuses to be a micromanager. The result is that their ministries mature and increase much faster.

And, finally, he encourages them to build relationships with other ministries and other teams. He understands that the team he leads, while it may be very strong in what it does, is not the only team that God is using to build His kingdom. When the team members are exposed to what other ministries and leadership teams are doing, they are able to glean some things that will benefit their own team. At the same time, they are able to impart some of what God is doing with them to the others. And in the rare instance where one of them should decide to change teams, it is probably God's way of shuffling the deck, so to speak, in order to place people where they will be used more effectively for the Kingdom. In either case, the result is a cross-pollination that greatly strengthens the overall work of the Kingdom!

When the team leader commissions and releases the others on the team, it not only strengthens and encourages them, personally, but it also allows them to breath something fresh into their own team that will help it to continue to grow and fulfill God's purposes for it. And, it nearly always bears the fruit of them becoming even more deeply committed to their own team.

In summary, if the team leader is a person of integrity, if he is continually allowing the fruit of the Spirit (Gal.5:22-23) to be developed in him, and if he genuinely desires to have a peer-level team around him, he will do everything that he possibly can to see that happen and to make sure that it functions properly and effectively. He understands that he is the key to making it work. Also, the example he sets in the areas set out in this chapter will be reflected in the other members of the team.

Chapter 8
Is He Worth Following?

In order for a peer-level team to function properly, the team leader should be responsible to the other members of the team in certain areas, and there are also areas in which the other team members should be responsible to him. Since the leader is the primary key to creating and maintaining a peer-level team, I will begin with some of the most important things that the rest of the team members should be able to expect from him.

THAT HE WOULD CAST VISION

The team leader is called to be the initial and primary vision caster for the team and for the ministry that he and the other team members oversee. When God calls someone to lead a ministry, He gives that person the foundational components of the vision that He has for that particular ministry. But it does not stop there; God also reveals more of the vision to him as time goes by. Vision that comes from God is always progressively revealed, meaning that God will not give the founding leader the entire vision all at once and in full detail. Why? Because God has also put vision in the hearts of other leaders that He desires to use to build upon the vision given to the founder of the ministry once they are brought together to form the team that will lead and oversee that ministry. As God then gathers those other leaders around that primary vision given to the founder of the ministry, the vision for the ministry becomes increasingly complete.

When I was growing up, I frequently saw my Grandmother Bernard working jigsaw puzzles, and as I got older I would try to help. Her system (like it is for many people who work jigsaw puzzles) was to find all of the edge pieces first and then fit them together to form the frame within which the rest of the puzzle would take shape. Back then, the puzzles were all square or rectangular (unlike many of the differently shaped puzzles of today), so it was easier to identify the edge pieces. But I noticed that even when the edge was complete, it looked very little like the picture on the box that the puzzle came in. However, as the interior pieces were put in place, the picture became progressively clearer. I also quickly came to realize that the bigger, more complex puzzles had a lot more pieces, and it took longer to complete them. I believe that the Lord gives the team leader (usually the founder of the ministry) a glimpse at the picture on the box, then He begins presenting him with the edge pieces of the vision. Meanwhile, God is gathering around the team leader those to whom He is giving the pieces that make up the rest of the puzzle. Some pictures require more pieces and, therefore, must be brought together by more team members. These puzzles (visions) take longer to complete than others, but they are worth the effort invested and the time required to see them finished. As the Bible says in Habakkuk 2:3 (NAS), "For the vision is yet for the appointed time; it hastens toward the goal and it will not fail. Though it tarries, wait for it; for it will certainly come, it will not delay." It is the responsibility of the team leader to keep the vision (the picture on the box) fresh and alive for the rest of the team members so that they will keep adding their pieces to it, thus completing the picture.

  If, for some reason, the original leader is no longer on the team, God will then impart the vision to the one whom He chooses to take his place, and as He does so He will quite often enlarge upon the original vision. Again, vision is progressively revealed, therefore it naturally continues to grow regardless of who the team leader may be. Every team leader, then, should be looking for the one who will eventually take his place, he should impart the vision to him as he currently sees it, and he should mentor him and challenge him to take the vision to ever newer levels. For example, when Joel Osteen took over the ministry that his dad,

John, had begun many years earlier, the vision did not only grow, it multiplied under his leadership. A vision that is truly from God will always be bigger than the initial team can fulfill in its lifetime!

THAT HE WOULD BE COMMITTED

The team leader must personally believe in having a peer-level team around him, he must have a sincere desire to see it formed, and he must be fully committed to do everything in his power to make it work. If not, it will not happen. Again, the leader is the key. If he is only willing to experiment with it and see if it works while not fully embracing the vision of the team being peer-level, it will have little chance of success. But if he is fully committed to seeing it happen, he will press through the challenges that are sure to come. If he is like most leaders who have never ministered with a team like this, he will find himself breaking new ground. In doing so, he will be required to make personal sacrifices to see it happen, and he will need to help the other team members find their way as the team begins to take shape.

In October of 1941, England was embroiled in its war with Germany, and the nation was suffering greatly from bombings, shortages of every kind, and the loss of many lives. On the 29th of that month, according to winstonchurchill.org, Prime Minister Winston Churchill gave a speech at Harrow School (which he had attended in his youth) in which he said, "Never give in. Never give in. Never, never, never, never — in nothing, great or small, large or petty — never give in, except to convictions of honor and good sense." His determination and commitment throughout the war was a great inspiration to the people of Britain. Similarly, if the members of a peer-level team are confident that their leader believes in what they are doing and is willing to see it through to fruition, they will also make every effort to see it happen. If the leader **never** gives up, he will inspire the other members to make the same commitment, and a very effective team will be formed.

THAT HE WOULD BE A TRAILBLAZER

Early in my ministry I saw myself as a trailblazer (someone who makes a path where no path existed before), and I made a commitment to continue blazing trails for as long as I could (figuratively speaking) pick up a machete and cut away whatever vegetation stood in the way of where I knew God would have me go. I made this commitment because I realized that by blazing a trail I would be opening up a way, not only for me to go to new places in God, but also to allow those who would come behind me to be able to get to those same places more easily. I also came to understand that if I were to stop blazing the trails, I would put more of a burden on the leaders who would come after me. They would not only have their own trails to blaze, but they would also have to finish the trails I did not complete. In order to blaze as many trails as possible I plan to continue in ministry, in one form or another, until the Lord takes me home.

The team leader should be a trailblazer, one who is not only willing to go first, but also one who is personally motivated to set an example for the other team members to follow. He should be one who understands that it is impossible to lead from behind. I am not saying that he should DO everything first. There will always be areas of ministry in which the Lord will involve others on the team, and the leader will never touch those areas because they are not a part of his calling. He must, however, set the example of faith-filled (often, sacrificial) obedience to what he has been called to do, both as an individual and as the team leader. This is very inspiring to the other members of the team as they, too, seek to fulfill their callings and the responsibilities that have been placed upon each of them, especially when that fulfillment requires them to take bold steps of faith.

However, he should never ask that they follow him blindly. In 1Cor.11:1 (NIV) Paul gives this challenge, "Follow my example, as I follow the example of Christ." The team leader should ask and expect the rest of the team members to follow his lead only so far as he is following after Christ!

THAT HE WOULD BE APPROACHABLE

The other team members must also know that their leader is open to receive input from them. In fact, they must be confident that he also *desires* their input. If the team leader presents himself as disinterested, he sends a message to the other team members that he does not really see them as his peers. If he is pre-occupied with something else when one of them is talking to him, if he negatively reacts when he is being lovingly confronted about an area in his life that needs adjustment, if he immediately dismisses a suggestion without even considering it, or if he in any way displays a condescending attitude toward those trying to give him input, he presents himself as being unapproachable. This causes the team members to feel excluded from him rather than feeling included by him.

There are many ways that a leader can show the other team members that he is approachable. For example, he should let their calls go to voicemail **only** if it is impossible for him to answer, and then he should return their calls as soon as it is practically feasible for him to do so. He should respond to their texts and e-mails as soon as possible. He can also do things like asking them for prayer in areas that he needs guidance, or in areas where he is struggling personally. He can seek their counsel in some areas of his personal life where he is seeking direction. Or he can give them the liberty to come to him if they think they see something about him that he may not be seeing. But I believe that the most effective way for him to make himself accessible is by spending as much one-on-one time with them as possible. I appreciate that, even though we live several hundred miles apart, my team leader always tries to find an opportunity to spend some personal time with me whenever we are together in the same geographical area.

A good team leader is approachable.

THAT HE WOULD VALUE THE OTHERS ON THE TEAM

A team leader must truly value the other members of his team and look for ways that he can demonstrate to them just how important they are to him. This does not necessarily mean that he frequently gives them gifts or praises them in front of large crowds (although those kinds of things should be done occasionally). Instead, he should show his appreciation for them in ways that may go unnoticed by others, but that mean a lot to the recipient. For example, as I was preparing to leave on one of my ministry trips out of the country, my team leader called to ask me more about the trip and to tell me that he was praying for me. This kind of thoughtfulness on his part was very encouraging to me and reinforced my confidence that he saw value in me.

As I discussed in the previous section, the leader can demonstrate how much he values the other team members by making himself easily available to them. If they are confident that he is immediately accessible, or that he will respond to them as soon as possible when he is not available at the moment, they know that they are important to him.

Another way to show that he values them is to do his best to be aware of what is happening in each of their families and to make a point of inquiring about those things from time to time, especially if something significant (whether positive or negative) is taking place. Back in the late 1980's when my family was going through a very difficult time, both of the key leaders of my team contacted my wife and me as soon as they heard about what was going on, and they stayed in contact with us through the most difficult days. One of them even made a special trip to come and be with us to pray with us and encourage us.

And finally, he should be inclusive in the way that he speaks *to* them and *about* them. For example, if good things are accomplished by the team, he should use the word "we" or "they" (and not the word "I") when talking about those things. In other words, he should not take the credit (hog the glory) for those accomplishments. He should also use the word "we" and not the word "you" when addressing the team regarding mistakes that have been made. By doing these things, he reinforces that he believes in the team and that they are all in it together, for better or for worse.

These are but a few of the ways whereby the team leader can demonstrate that he values the team members, not only for what they do, but also for who they are. These should be some of the things that he does for them on a regular basis.

THAT HE WOULD BE ACCOUNTABLE

The team members must also know that their leader not only believes in accountability, but he practices it himself. This means three things. First, he makes himself truly accountable to the Lord by keeping his heart tender and open to the dealings of the Holy Spirit in his own life. When the other team members see his deepening relationship with the Lord and the resulting changes that become obvious in his life, they know that he is making himself accountable to the Lord.

Second, he makes himself accountable to those to whom he looks for spiritual oversight (which, of course, implies that he has someone like that in his life). When I became the senior pastor of Living Word Church, I understood the principle of making oneself accountable to others for spiritual oversight, but there was something of an independent spirit in my heart that made me resist doing that. Yet, if I was going to ask the people in the church to make themselves accountable to me, I knew that I should at least give the appearance of being a man under authority. Therefore, I let it be known that I made myself accountable to Earl Kellum, an apostolic missionary in Mexico to whom my father had looked for spiritual oversight when he was senior pastor. I had known him for many years, and I had a very good relationship with him, and so did the church. However, deep down inside, I knew that he did not come our way very often and that he would rarely give me input unless I asked for it, so naming him as my spiritual oversight meant that I could say I was under authority while still maintaining my personal autonomy. As a consequence, I found it difficult to get others to become accountable to me as their pastor and spiritual leader. It was only after I repented of my hypocrisy and made myself genuinely accountable to Bro. Kellum and to others as my spiritual oversight that I began to see a turnaround in the church. I finally understood that, in order to have authority, I must also be under authority. The Roman centurion whom Jesus encountered in Matthew chapter 8 understood how this principle works when he asked Jesus to heal his servant simply by commanding it to be done. Believe me, the members of the team will be able to discern whether or not their leader is truly accountable to his own spiritual oversight!

And third, he makes himself accountable to the other team members. Although they are not those whom he looks to for spiritual oversight, he should be willing to submit his character and his actions to them. Since the members of the team are usually in closer proximity to their leader than are his overseers, they will probably be the first to see any potential behavioral problems or negative character issues in him. Making himself accountable to them means that he invites and welcomes their input in these areas.

A team leader who expects accountability from the members of his team will also make himself accountable. He will be accountable to the Lord, he will be accountable to his spiritual overseers, and he will be accountable to those on his team.

THAT HE WOULD MAKE PROVISION FOR APPEALS

Sometimes, team members will have a disagreement with their leader that seemingly cannot be resolved, or the leader may make a decision (from which he refuses to budge) that others on the team feel is wrong. When one of these things happens, all of the members of the team should know that they have a right to appeal. This means that the team leader has already made it known that, should such a situation arise, the other team members have the liberty to contact those to whom the leader looks for his oversight in order to ask them to evaluate the problem and to provide a solution. In fact, the leader should encourage them to do so. This is a safeguard both for them and for him, because the input received from those giving oversight should clarify things for everyone involved. When all parties are willing to abide by the decision of the ones who oversee the team leader, issues can be resolved without causing any bitterness.

Now, obviously, exercising that right should be reserved for only the most serious of disagreements. Minor issues should be resolved within the team context. But the problem with not having that policy in place is that the team leader would be implying that he sees himself as the final authority and that anyone disagreeing with him would have no choice but to submit or be considered rebellious. The lack of an avenue for appeal would eventually create wounds that would probably fester to the point that disunity would begin to grow. If, however, he has already instituted the policy of the right to appeal, problems can be avoided.

By instituting this policy, the leader acknowledges that he could be wrong at times and that he will change his position should it become necessary. And by accepting the policy, the other members of the team are committing themselves to submit to the decision made by the overseers should it be determined that they are the ones in the wrong.

THAT HE WOULD PUBLICLY SUPPORT THE MEMBERS OF THE TEAM

I am sure that we have all played the "blame game" from time to time. We usually do it because we don't want to look bad in front of others or because we don't want to get into trouble and suffer the consequences of our misbehavior. So, we either blame someone else outright or we "creatively" explain things in a way that gives the impression that the bad thing that happened was not really our fault. Either way, we are trying to avoid taking responsibility for a problem that has occurred. It is not surprising that this kind of behavior is frequently found in children, but it is a sad thing when it is discovered in our leaders. Unfortunately, it happens far too often, not only with those from whom we have begun to expect it (like many politicians, sadly), but with many of our spiritual leaders as well.

Obviously, if a team leader messes up in a way that has corporate consequences, he should confess it publicly, ask forgiveness, and seek restoration. Any attempt on his part to cover it up, to justify it, or to make excuses for what he did will cause those he leads to lose confidence in him and in the team as a whole.

But from time to time, a member of the team may make an unintentional mistake that affects the whole team in a negative way; or sometimes, the entire team will make a decision that backfires, producing unforeseen negative consequences. Both scenarios tend to reflect badly upon the team leader. If one of these happens, he should be very careful not to play the blame game in order to deflect that negativity from himself. This kind of response is extremely destructive to a peer-level team, because the members of the team feel betrayed by their leader when he "hangs them out to dry" in this manner. Instead, he should acknowledge the problem by admitting that a mistake was made, and, whether it was done by one individual or by the team as a whole, he should use the words "we" and "I" when addressing the situation. The way he deals with it should convey the message, "We have failed you, and I take personal responsibility for it." When Harry S. Truman was serving as President of the Unite States, he had a sign on his desk that read, "The Buck Stops Here." When a team leader publicly takes that kind of position, he shows the rest of the team that he "has their backs."

In addition to properly dealing with the negatives, he should also make a commitment to always speak positively about the other members of the team when he is outside of the team meetings. The place for problems to be addressed and differences to be reconciled is within the meetings or in one-on-one discussions. Sometimes, problems take some time to resolve, and the delay can be very frustrating for the leader who wants everything to flow smoothly. But he should make sure that he never shares this privileged information with someone who is neither a part of the problem nor a part of the solution. Outside of the meetings, he should only speak well of the others on the team. If he disciplines himself to mentally dwell mainly on their good qualities instead of those that he finds to be less than favorable, this will not be a problem for him.

THAT HE WOULD BE A MOTIVATOR

I'm sure we hate to admit it, but all of us are still a lot like children in many ways, and one of those ways is that we all need regular motivation in our lives. We should all be self-motivated to some degree (Some of us are better at it than others.), but we also need the motivation that others give us. That's not a bad thing, it's just the way we are. Without motivation we would never accomplish anything.

The team leader should realize that one of his responsibilities to the other team members is to regularly motivate them in ways that will help them achieve their fullest potential, not only in relationship to the team, but also in their personal lives, in their family relationships, and in their own callings and ministries. There are three primary ways he can do this.

One of the best ways team members can be motivated is by giving them praise and recognition whenever it is warranted. This should regularly be bestowed upon them both in a personal one-on-one setting, and also in the corporate team context. It should even be given publically from time to time. When this happens, the recipient is not only thankful that the leader noticed what was done, but he is also encouraged to continue to strive for excellence in all of his endeavors.

The next way that the leader can motivate the team is to challenge them to reach beyond where they are currently, both personally and in their ministries. He can do this by opening doors for them that will allow them to experience new things and by giving them new responsibilities that will utilize and further develop their personal gifts and talents. When I started making ministry trips to Mexico, I spent a lot of time with Earl Kellum, a long-time missionary there and one of the people to whom I looked for spiritual oversight. Every time I was there, he went out of his way to make sure that I preached in as many churches as possible, and he included me in almost everything he did with the pastors and leaders. This opened doors of ministry and relationships for me that I never could have opened on my own, all of which are still a blessing to me today.

Another pastor and personal mentor of mine by the name of Hong Sit also challenged me in my early days of ministry. Even though I had known for several years that God was calling me into full-time ministry, by the time Cindy and I got married I was rejecting that call and planning to be a college professor, instead. When we moved to Houston, Texas, in 1970 so that I could work on my Master's Degree in English Literature at the University of Houston, we decided that we should find a church to attend. After visiting several churches we felt drawn to Grace Chapel, a church that was made up of about one-half Chinese Americans and the other half Anglos. Dr. Hong Sit was the pastor there, and he quickly recognized God's call on my life and began challenging me to ever greater responsibilities in the church. During the five and one-half years that Cindy and I were there, I progressed from being worship leader, to youth leader, to deacon, to elder, and finally to being his assistant pastor. Each challenge further utilized and developed the gifts and talents that were in me, and because Pastor Sit encouraged me in this way, I returned to the call of God on my life.

The third way that the leader can motivate the others is through giving them correction when it is needed. When we hear that term, we often think about *punishment*, but that is not at all what I am talking about here. Instead, what I am referring to is a leader who cares enough about the other members of the team that he is willing to challenge them when he sees them getting off course and he is willing to help them make corrections so that they can stay on the right track. When I am driving somewhere I have not been before, I often use a GPS navigation device to help me find my way. The one I use warns me when I miss a turn or somehow get off course, and then it gives me a way to get back on course. Sometimes I have to turn around and go back the way I came, and sometimes, if I have strayed significantly, it charts an altogether different course for me to follow that will take me to my destination. This is the kind of correction that motivates. Team members who receive it from their leader, even if they do not initially like it, will eventually thank him for it.

THAT HE WOULD EMPOWER THE TEAM MEMBERS

I once spent some time on staff with a pastor who freely gave out responsibilities to his team, but he always required them to clear everything with him prior to implementing any decisions they made regarding what he asked them to do. He meant well. He desired to avoid as many mistakes as possible, and he wanted things done the "right" way. What he failed to realize, however, was that he was giving out assignments without empowering the team members to properly and effectively carry out those tasks. This was very frustrating to his staff members because they were also good leaders in their own right. It made them feel like they were simply hired help, and it caused them to believe that their leader did not really trust them. If he had been told this, he would have responded that he did, indeed, trust them to carry out his wishes --- he just believed that he knew the best way of getting those things done.

A good team leader should understand that the delegation of responsibilities to someone must also include the delegation of the authority necessary to make the decisions that will have to be made in order to carry out those responsibilities. He should understand that it would be correct for him to define the parameters within which that person is to operate, and that it would be proper to hold that person accountable to operate within those parameters with integrity and in a manner that would stay true to the vision of the team. However, he must allow that person the liberty to complete those responsibilities in the way that person thinks is best (even though it will probably not be the way the team leader would do it). This kind of empowerment on the part of the team leader instills confidence in the team members by letting them know that he truly does trust them. Will mistakes be made along the way? Of course. But usually the final results are far better than they would have been had the team members not been empowered in this way.

Empowering also involves making sure that each team member works in the area or areas best suited to him. In order for this to happen, the leader must recognize each member's spiritual gifts, ministry gifts, and individual strengths and weaknesses. He should accomplish this, not only by spending quality time with each of them, but also by praying regularly for them and asking the Lord to show him what He has deposited in each one of them. Pastor Sit, whom I mentioned earlier, was very good at doing this; he saw gifts, callings, and potential strengths in me that I was either denying or not yet recognizing, and he helped me develop them by challenging me to repeatedly take on new responsibilities in the church. Even though a team member will usually be willing to try to do whatever is asked of him, he will be the most effective and will feel the most personal satisfaction if he is asked to function in an area that best utilizes his dominant gifts and his greatest strengths (or potential strengths). A team member who is working outside of his element can become very frustrated and ineffective by trying to be faithful in an area where he simply does not fit well.

When the team leader accepts these responsibilities (and whatever others the Lord may show him), he lays the proper foundation upon which a peer-level team can be built. It also sets an example for the other team members to follow as they, in turn, make themselves responsible to him.

Chapter 9
Are They Worth Leading?

On a peer-level team, responsibilities go both ways. There are not only certain things that the team members should be able to expect from their leader, but there are also things that the leader should be able to expect from the other members of the team. In order for the team to function properly, the members should understand and faithfully perform the responsibilities that they carry in relationship to their leader and to each other. In this chapter we will examine some of the most important ones.

THAT THEY WOULD BE COMMITTED TO THE VISION OF THE TEAM

This should go without saying. However, there may occasionally be someone on the team who claims to be committed to the team vision when, in reality, his real commitment is to his own agenda, and he hopes to use the team relationships to help promote that agenda. He sees the vision of the team as a springboard to help him launch his own vision and as something that will help him fulfill his own personal goals instead of the other way around. This is nothing less than betrayal, and sooner or later the offender will be exposed. Unless that person repents, he should be removed from the team so that the vision of the team is not compromised. A tragic Biblical example of this is seen in the life of Absalom who used his position in his father David's kingdom to undermine the king and temporarily take part of the kingdom away from him. Sadly, many ministry leaders and local church pastors have had similar experiences where people joined their teams under the pretense of wanting to help, then proceeded to use their positions to undermine the leaders in such a way as to cause great damage to the ministry and deep wounds to the leaders. I related, in great detail, a true story of an occurrence such as this in chapter 25 ("Unfriendly Fire") of my book, The Jefe Factor. In brief, one of the elders of a small church asked for and received the blessing of the pastor and the other elders to spend a few months helping the pastor of an even smaller church in another city build up his church. The first Sunday he was to be gone, however, he started a new church just a few miles from the church where he was still considered an elder, and he took about one half of the congregation with him! This kind of thing should never happen!

Now, obviously, a good leadership team will be made up of people who, in their own right, are all strong leaders. As such, they will carry their own visons with them when they join the team; however, they should value the vision of the team more highly than they do their own. In other words, they need to understand that the visions they bring with them should be used to help fulfill and enhance the vision of the team. If they can understand that their visions were given to them for the purpose of being part of a much larger vision, they will discover that their own visions have the potential to experience a higher level of fulfillment, and to have a greater impact as part of that bigger vision, than they ever would have had apart from the team relationship.

This is one of the things that I appreciate about the ICLC team of which I am a part. All of us team members are strong leaders who carry with us our own very clear visions, but we have submitted our own visions to the larger vision of the team. We have come to understand that, by doing so, our personal visions have now become integral parts of "orchestrating a world-wide penetration of the Gospel" (the vision of the team). And we are all seeing a greater fulfillment of our own visions as a result. For example, I had been making ministry trips to Mexico to help encourage and strengthen the churches and leaders there long before I became a part of the ICLC team. But after becoming part of that team, I found that there was not only a greater anointing on my own ministry in Mexico, but that I was also able to involve other team members in my ministry there, thus adding a much broader dimension to it than I ever could have accomplished by myself. And because of my relationship to the ICLC team, my personal vision for strengthening and encouraging leaders has expanded and taken me into several other nations around the world! When a strong leader is willing to submit his own visions to the larger vision of a peer-level team, it is beneficial both to him and to the team as a whole.

THAT THEY WOULD RECOGNIZE FINAL AND EMERGENCY AOUTHORITY

Let me say again that a peer-level leadership team is not the same thing as a co-equal leadership team. Even though the team leader should treat the other team members as his peers, they must in turn allow and expect him to exercise final and emergency authority. Please let me explain what I mean by final and emergency authority.

The process of making decisions for a peer-level team should begin with an open and honest discussion of an issue during which each member feels free to give his or her input, and the discussion should be bathed in prayer. At the end of the prayerful discussion, if every member (including the leader) is agreed as to what the decision should be, then the matter is settled. If, however, even one of the members is not in agreement, the leader should postpone a decision on the matter until everyone has had more time to further pray over it. When it is discussed again, if there is still not an agreement on the issue, the team members must recognize that the leader has the authority to make a decision regarding the matter regardless of whether that decision agrees with the majority or with the minority. This is what I mean by final authority. If any of the team members strongly disagree with his decision, they have the right to appeal (which was addressed in the last chapter), and whether or not they decide to appeal, they should continue to maintain the spirit of agreement which was described in chapter 4 of this book.

Occasionally, a situation will arise which will require that an immediate decision be made. If there is enough time, the leader should try to contact as many members of the team as possible in order to get their input on the matter, but whether or not he is able to do so, it should be recognized that he has the authority to make the required decision. This is what I mean by emergency authority. This should never be a problem for the rest of the team members because, if the peer-level team is functioning properly, they will know the heart of their leader, and they will trust him fully in such instances. As soon as possible after the emergency decision has been made, however, the leader should inform the rest of the team members of what he has done so that everyone is aware of what happened and so that no one finds out about it in an unexpected way.

THAT THEY WOULD BE DEPENDABLE AND ACCOUNTABLE

One of the things that most frustrates a team leader is a team member who does not follow through with his responsibilities. If a team member accepts a responsibility for which he is clearly suited and fully capable of performing, he should be faithful to carry it out to the best of his ability. Quite often, fulfilling the commitment will cost him more than he realized it would when he agreed to take it on. In Psalm 15 David describes the kind of person who stands firm. One characteristic (v.4, NIV) is that he "keeps an oath even when it hurts." This is where a person's dependability is proven. Anyone can follow through on his responsibilities when it is easy to do so. When a team member faithfully fulfills his responsibilities (even when it hurts), it is VERY encouraging, not only to the leader, but also to the rest of the team.

Therefore, not only does the team leader need to recognize each member's callings and strengths (as I discussed in the previous chapter), but each member should also seek to be aware of his own abilities and limitations, as well as those of the other members. This awareness helps assure that each person is properly placed and that he can be counted on to function well in his area(s) of responsibility.

A key ingredient to fulfilling a responsibility is accountability. When a member assumes a responsibility, he should make himself accountable to the leader and to the rest of the team regarding how he is performing in that area. This is best done by giving regular reports to the team about what is happening, what has been happening, and what is planned to happen in the future, and then by allowing the rest of the team to give him feedback. This not only keeps him accountable, but it keeps the lines of communication open with the leader and the rest of the team. It also serves to make everyone more aware of what the others are doing, thereby including them in everything that is happening.

THAT THEY WOULD BE TEACHABLE

Have you ever known teen-agers who always say, "I know," when you try to tell them something? Annoying, isn't it? After a while you probably decided to quit trying to advise them and to let them find out the hard way that they should have listened to you in the first place. A lot of teens go through a period like that in their lives. It is very frustrating, not only for their parents, but also for others who should be allowed to give them some much-needed input. While most of them eventually outgrow it, some stay that way into adulthood. And when someone like that finds his way onto a peer-level team, it is frustrating for everyone on the team, especially the leader.

Now, it is usually more difficult to identify this attitude with adults. Instead of saying "I know," they usually appear to be listening to what is being said, and they may even express agreement with it. Afterward, however, they go ahead and do whatever they want to do. But at some point, their unwillingness to receive input and to be teachable becomes evident, especially when nothing changes. Even though they may have smiled while receiving the input, inwardly they were arrogantly dismissing what was being said, maybe even feeling offended by it. In fact, arrogance is the main reason why many people have an unteachable spirit.

I have to confess that I learned this the hard way. Several times in my first thirty years of full-time ministry, different people tried to address some character issues in my life that genuinely needed correction. Each time someone tried to point these out to me, I would smile and thank him for his input, but inwardly my response was usually something like, "Who do you think you are to try to tell me what I should do!" Arrogant? Absolutely. And it was not until I experienced a series of severe setbacks, both in ministry and in business, that I came to the place that God was able to show me my arrogance and to help me repent of it. Now, thankfully, I am much more teachable!

A member of a peer-level team who is approachable and teachable is a blessing because he takes to heart the input given him and becomes a better person and team member because of it. However, an unteachable member creates frustration in the other members of the team, because his refusal to receive input prevents him from growing and improving, both in the responsibilities he carries and also in his personal life. This, at the very least, impedes the effectiveness of the team as a whole, and at worst, it can cause credibility problems for the team. I know someone who was unapproachable and unteachable regarding some serious character flaws in his life, and these flaws eventually hurt a lot of people, both personally and financially. And because he was a key part of a leadership team at the time, the resulting fallout severely damaged the team's reputation for many years afterward. Proverbs 12:1 (NKJV) says, "Whoever loves instruction loves knowledge, but he who hates correction is stupid." I guess that sums it up pretty nicely!

THAT THEY WOULD APPROACH PERSONAL ISSUES RESPECTFULLY

Now, everyone has areas in their personal lives that could be improved upon. And whenever people work closely together for an extended period of time, personal issues are going to surface. The more time we spend with each other, the more obvious those things become.

And while some of those issues can be annoying to others, they may not be serious enough to address. However, if those issues begin to negatively affect that person's ministry, or if they begin to cause his relationship with the other team members or with people outside the team to suffer, he should be confronted regarding those issues. But the manner in which that person is approached is extremely important.

First of all, in Matthew 18:15-17 (NIV), Jesus gives very clear direction regarding the process that should be followed. "If your brother or sister sins, go and point out their fault, just between the two of you. If they listen to you, you have won them over. But if they will not listen, take one or two others along, so that 'every matter may be established by the testimony of two or three witnesses.' If they still refuse to listen, tell it to the church; and if they refuse to listen even to the church, treat them as you would a pagan or a tax collector." We should not, however, be so eager to follow the process that we neglect the spirit in which that person should be addressed. Paul gives us understanding of how this should be done in Galatians 6:1 (NIV) where he writes, "Brothers and sisters, if someone is caught in a sin, you who live by the Spirit should restore that person gently. But watch yourselves, or you also may be tempted."

Putting these scriptures together gives us a good picture of how the issues should be addressed, whether they be in the team leader or in other members of the team. The person who feels the need to address an issue should first examine himself to make sure that his motives are pure. In other words, he should make sure that he has no other agenda besides genuinely wanting to help that person and sincerely wanting to see that person restored from weakness to strength. Then, he should make sure that he is being led by the Spirit as to when and how to approach that person; timing and setting are critical. He should approach that person with a servant's heart and a submissive spirit (especially if he is addressing the team leader), and he should do it privately and not publicly. If these steps are followed, the rest of the process that Jesus gives will rarely have to be utilized. But if does become necessary to involve others, it should be done in the same spirit by everyone involved.

THAT THEY WOULD DISCUSS EVERYTHING OPENLY

Many years ago, when I was the pastor of a church in Texas, some of my leadership team became concerned about the direction in which the church was going. However, instead of openly bringing their concerns to the leadership meetings, they began to talk among themselves in private. They soon decided that I was the cause of the misdirection and that they needed to pray that I would come to an understanding of things the way they saw them. In other words, they believed that they had better insight as to how to lead the church than I did, but they had yet to talk with me about it.

As time went by, I began to sense that something was obviously wrong. Even though none of them had said anything negative to me, I had the nagging feeling that the others on my leadership team were constantly reaching "down" to me in an effort to try to help me in some way. Other than that, I was clueless as to what was going on. They finally became so frustrated with not seeing the changes they desired to see that they decided on another course of action; they asked me if they could contact some men that I looked to for spiritual oversight and ask them for input about some vaguely defined issues, all the while without talking openly with me about any of their concerns. Still in the dark, I agreed for them to do so because I had total confidence in the integrity and spiritual discernment that these men possessed.

Not long afterward, these men asked me if they could meet with me and the other church leaders in order to address some problems they saw in our church. Of course I agreed, still not knowing what had been going on behind my back. When we all came together for the meeting, one of these men very graciously began to identify the problem as emanating, not from me, but from one of the women on the team who had been subtly manipulating the other members of the team to the point that they believed that there was something wrong with me. It was a manifestation of the spirit of Jezebel. As he explained what the issue really was, I finally realized why I had been feeling the way I had. But then I saw something else happening as he talked; I literally saw the countenance of each person change. It was like a light bulb came on over each one's head! And then a genuine miracle took place: the truth set them free, they all repented of what they had done (including the lady whom this spirit had been influencing), and their attitude toward me changed immediately! Literally overnight, I could sense a difference; instead of feeling that they were trying to "reach down" to help me come up to their level, I felt fully supported by each of them. Only sometime later did one of these men who addressed the issue tell me that when he first became aware of what was happening with these leaders, he believed that the problem was so serious that he doubted that the church would survive!

I thank God that my leaders called on these men who had the discernment to see the root of the problem and who had the grace to address it properly. I was also extremely grateful that the spirit of revelation fell in that place, and that my church leaders were willing to respond in the right spirit. As a result, we did not lose even one person from the church, and the leadership team became even stronger than ever before!

In a peer-level team, everything must be discussed openly and honestly. Otherwise, dissension and possibly even division are sure to occur. Obviously, there will be times when a member becomes concerned with the direction in which the team is moving or with some other issue regarding the team. THESE CONCERNS SHOULD BE ADDRESSED OPENLY! When everything is exposed to the light, all darkness has to flee!

THAT THEY WOULD HONOR THE LEADER AND EACH OTHER

Honor is a word that has almost fallen into disuse in many cultures today. It seems that the more advanced a society becomes, the less it tends to value the principle of giving honor where honor is due (Rom.13:7, NASB). Perhaps it is a by-product of the self-centeredness that tends to accompany prosperity. But whatever the reason, it is something that should not be lost, especially in the church culture. Summarizing Dictionary.com, giving honor where honor is due means to show high respect for someone who acts with honesty, fairness, or integrity. In reality, the most important thing that we should hope to see demonstrated in others are these qualities. And when we do see them, we should not only *feel* an appreciation of what we see, but we should also find opportunities to *express* that appreciation openly. I know of a church that periodically chooses to honor someone who faithfully serves the church in a behind-the-scenes capacity by publicly giving that person a t-shirt that says "unsung hero" and by expressing appreciation for what he or she does for the church.

This principle of honor is very important in a peer-level team relationship. It is essential, not only that each of the members be honorable in his own right, but also that he regularly expresses his appreciation when he sees his leader and others on the team acting honorably. This expression should happen both within the team setting and also publically. By honoring them in this way, he is openly and freely expressing his support for each of them.

Giving honor where honor is due is something that keeps the team members properly focused in their relationship with each other because in so doing, each one's positive characteristics are emphasized instead of the negative. It is a practical application of Phil.4:8 (NIV) where Paul says, "Finally, brothers and sisters, whatever is true, whatever is noble, whatever is right, whatever is pure, whatever is lovely, whatever is admirable—if anything is excellent or praiseworthy—think about such things." This not only encourages the one being honored to continue being honorable, but it also has a positive impact on the people who are a part of the ministry that this team leads. When they see that kind of honor being expressed, they develop a greater level of confidence in the team as a whole, and especially in the leader.

THAT THEY WOULD FAITHFULLY PRAY FOR THE LEADER AND FOR EACH OTHER

The old hymn, "What a Friend We Have in Jesus" includes this phrase:

> *O what peace we often forfeit,*
> *O what needless pain we bear,*
> *All because we do not carry*
> *Everything to God in prayer!*

When the members of a peer-level team regularly and consistently pray for each other and for their leader, good things happen! Why? First, because prayer allows God to change things by changing us. It amazes me how often when I have been praying for God to do something in somebody else's life, that He changes me instead. And sometimes after He changes me, I realize that I was the problem all along. Or if I discover that the other person genuinely needs to be changed, I can then pray for him the way that God wants me to, thus making my prayers much more effective.

Prayer is also a means of supporting each other in our respective ministries. Every time I go to other nations to minister, I solicit prayer support from as many people as possible, but especially from my wife and from those who are my team members. They know me better than anyone else, and they know how to intercede on my behalf. As a result, I am not only covered spiritually by them as I go, but I also minster more effectively as a result of their prayers. I believe that this is the kind of prayer support that Paul had in mind when he wrote in Rom.15:30 (NIV), "I urge you, brothers and sisters, by our Lord Jesus Christ and by the love of the Spirit, to join me in my struggle by praying to God for me."

Again, when we pray for each other good things happen!

When the team members accept these responsibilities and others that the Lord shows them, they strengthen the foundation upon which their team is built. It becomes like the house built upon the rock that Jesus talks about in Matthew 7:24-25. The storms that always come in one form or another will not destroy the team!

Chapter 10
Foundation Stones

When the construction of a new multi-storied building begins, the first thing that must be put in place is a proper foundation. The taller the building, the stronger and usually deeper the foundation must be. The manner in which the foundation is constructed is determined by the conditions of the upper layer of soil and by the stability of the various lower layers. The Torre Latino Americana building in Mexico City was built in the early 1950's. It incorporated a foundation system which utilizes many very deep, almost spring-like, steel and concrete columns upon which the building rests. This design, innovative for its time, was created because of the unstable soil and the frequent earthquakes in that area. I remember once standing on the observation deck at the top of that very tall building, and I could feel it swaying back and forth a little bit in the wind. It was a bit unnerving, to say the least. But because of its excellent yet flexible foundation, it has remained undamaged by multiple earthquakes that have shaken Mexico City since its construction, even the 7.9 of 1957 and the 8.1 of 1985 which destroyed many buildings in that city.

In the same way, a peer-level team must be built upon a good foundation if it is to accomplish all that God has planned for the ministry or organization which it leads. A number of years, ago a very precious brother by the name of Philip Mohabir (who has since gone to be with the Lord) shared about the five things that he believed must be held in common by each member of a leadership team in order for it to function properly. In the years since I heard him share this, I have observed that the teams that applied these principles were much more effective in fulfilling their God-given purposes than those that did not. Therefore, I believe that these are the five most important foundation stones upon which a peer-level team must be built if it is to be everything that God intends it to be.

MANDATE

God has in His heart a specific purpose for every ministry that He brings into existence. It is imperative, therefore, that the leadership team knows exactly what this purpose is, and it is nearly always the one whom God calls to lead the team who will hear it the most clearly. This God-given purpose is a divine mandate that must be followed if the team wants to see the ministry it oversees accomplish all that God desires for it. This is the one foundation stone that must never change; it is the cornerstone to which everything else must connect. Without it, there is no standard by which to evaluate everything that could potentially become part of the ministry as it develops and moves forward. With it, there is a clear directive that directs and evaluates every aspect of that ministry.

This mandate should then be summarized into some kind of a mission statement that clearly identifies the God-given purpose of that ministry to everyone who reads it. It should be clear enough to be easily understood, yet succinct enough to be easily remembered. For example, the mandate that God has given the leadership team of ICLC through our team leader, Sam Matthews, is summarized in the mission statement, "Orchestrating a World-wide Penetration of the Gospel." This has become the cornerstone to which everything must be connected if it is to be an integral part of the ministry of ICLC. Everyone on the team has embraced this as God's mandate for ICLC and for each of us, individually, as we serve on this team. This mandate burns in our hearts and compels us forward both as a team and as individuals as we function in our own respective ministries.

A clear mission statement which is developed out of a God-given mandate is essential for a peer-level team. It is something that must be held in common by each member of the team, and it must be followed whole-heartedly if the ministry is to fulfill its God-given purposes.

VISION

Vision is the Spirit-birthed anticipation of where the mandate will take the team and its ministry. Proverbs 29:18 states that where there is no vision the people perish, cast off restraint, get out of control, are scattered abroad, lose self-control, decay, run wild, stumble all over themselves, do whatever they want, are destroyed, or are made naked (according to the various translations of that verse). History clearly affirms that any or all of these things will happen when people have no vision. In fact, I see many of these characteristics in this present generation of young people. They have been so frequently warned of such things as climate change, a polluted atmosphere, possible nuclear war, domestic terrorism, overpopulation, and dwindling natural resources that many of them have no vision for any kind of a decent future. Consequently, it is not uncommon for them to adopt the attitude of "eat, drink, and be merry as much as possible right now" because they believe they have no future and no hope.

The same thing happens to a leadership team that has no clear, cohesive vision; both the team and the ministry that it leads will begin to perish, cast off restraint, etc. While each member of the team probably carries a vision for his own personal ministry, the team as a whole will only be effective when it has a vision that draws the members together with one heart to see that vision completed, and a vision that inspires each one of them to submit his personal vision to the corporate one in order for that to happen.

The vision, like the mandate, must be birthed in the heart of the Father; and, again like the mandate it is nearly always given first to the team leader. Now, I am not suggesting that he will receive it in its entirety, but he will be given the heart of it, and the other team members will be given additional parts of it that will help flesh it out, so to speak. For example, the team leader may be given a vision to help those functioning in the five-fold ministries in various parts of the world to network together in order to more effectively reach their spheres of influence by encouraging and equipping their local leaders and by establishing schools and other programs to train up others in ministry. While the leader will be burdened to see this happening in the geographic locations that God puts on his own heart, others on the team will desire to see it happening in other parts of the world. And each one of them will envision it happening in somewhat different ways than the others on the team. This is how the vision becomes more and more complete.

The vision must then be allowed to grow and change. **Whereas the mandate is unchangeable, the vision must be flexible.** Referring again to Proverbs 29:18, another translation of the Hebrew word used here for vision is progressive revelation. Every vision that God gives is revealed progressively; He never gives us the fullness of it all at once. Why? Because if He did, we would not be ready for it, and we would almost certainly mess it up in some way by trying to see it come to pass ahead of its time! On a recent visit to Changsha, China, a friend and I stayed in a nice hotel in an area that was a mixture of older residential apartments alongside the construction of large new buildings that would one day be filled with many prosperous businesses. As we walked around to see what was in the newer buildings near the hotel, we discovered that a lot of the commercial spaces had once housed some well-known names, but they were now standing empty. In fact, many of the spaces around there were unoccupied, but they showed evidence that they had housed businesses and shops of various kinds fairly recently. The businesses that did seem to be prospering were primarily those that catered to the middle-to-lower-income people who lived in the area; the higher-end stores had been forced to close. I believe this happened because of a vision out of season. Eventually, that area will probably support the higher-end stores, but those who saw the vision for the future and tried to make it happen too soon failed to see the fulfillment of it.

By not revealing everything at once, God is not trying to keep us in the dark, but He is showing us great mercy. Why? Because every vision requires a price to be paid in order for it to be fulfilled. If we knew ahead of time what would be required of us in doing our part in paying that price, I'm not sure how many of us would be willing to pursue it. Shortly after my wife and I moved to Durango, Colorado, in 1997, Cindy had a severe asthma attack, and she stopped breathing while I was rushing her to the nearby hospital. After treating her in the emergency room and admitting her to the hospital, the doctors told me that had we arrived any later she would have died or, at the very least, have suffered brain damage. She wound up staying there for several days as they continued to treat her and decide upon the best medications that would prevent another such occurrence (thank God, she has remained stable since then). On one of my frequent visits there to see her, I prayed as I was walking from the parking lot and asked, "God, why did this happen? We came here out of obedience to You, not out of rebellion of any kind. I don't understand." In my mind I immediately heard Him answer, "I just wanted to see if you were willing to pay the price." "Wow," I thought, "I'm glad that's over!" And in His mercy, He didn't correct me. However, after many years of walking out an intercession for the area which required us to pay a price that I probably would have run from had I known about it ahead of time, He finally showed me that the asthma attack was not the price. It was simply a test to see if we could be trusted to pay our part of the price which was required to see His vision for the area fulfilled. God, in His faithfulness, gives us progressive revelation as He prepares us to be able to embrace each installment of the vision at the proper time for it to happen.

VALUES

In Matthew 13:45-46 (NASB) Jesus says, "Again, the kingdom of heaven is like a merchant seeking fine pearls, and upon finding one pearl of great value, he went and sold all that he had and bought it." This is an excellent description of what it means to put value on something --- it means that it is worth making whatever sacrifices are necessary in order to acquire it. Obviously, we all have our own opinions of what is valuable, those things for which we are willing to make sacrifices. In addition to my personal relationship with the Lord, one of the things that I value most is my family. Over the years, I have made many personal sacrifices in order for them to have the best that I could give them in every area of their lives. And I regret none of those sacrifices. Why? Because they are precious to me!

In order for a peer-level team to be effective, each of its members must subscribe to the same set of core values. While each member will most likely have his own personal values, when it comes to the team as a whole, he should be in agreement with the values that the team embraces. In other words, each team member must believe that the mandate and the vision which the team carries are worth making whatever sacrifices are necessary in order to see them carried out. If this is not the case, the team will be divided regarding which sacrifices should be made. In a local church leadership team, for example, if some of the members wish to use the church's finances to build a large fancy building while others want to use those finances to send out more missionaries, that team will be dangerously divided. These kinds of disagreements usually arise because the mandate and vision have not been clearly defined, therefore people are joined to that team who carry differing expectations based upon what they each believe to be God's purposes for that ministry. While differing personal values are not necessarily wrong in themselves, differing core values cannot co-exist on the same leadership team.

When all the members of a team share the same core values, the team's mandate and vision will be accomplished much more effectively. For example, in order for there to be a world-wide penetration of the gospel, each member of our national leadership team for ICLC is willing to sacrifice to see it happen. We are willing to personally go to the nations where God sends us, we are doing everything we can to see future leaders trained, equipped, and mentored, and we are helping send out those whom God is calling to the nations. These activities, and others like them, require sacrifices of time and money, but we gladly do them because we all value the same things.

STRATEGY

All good military leaders and all successful coaches of athletic teams develop a very clear and specific strategy for how to win each battle or each game. And although that strategy will always contain some of the same elements in every application of it, it will be adjusted each time it is used, "tailor made" so to speak, in order for it to be the most effective it can be against the current opponent.

The same should be true for a peer-level leadership team. Strategy is a clear and specific practical application of the vision. Without strategy, vision is only a nice dream that everyone hopes will happen some day, one of those "wouldn't it be nice if" scenarios that never becomes a reality. With proper strategy, the vision can and will be accomplished!

There are five key things that must be understood about strategy in order for it to be effective. First, and foremost, the strategy employed must never require those involved to violate the principles of the Word of God or their personal convictions regarding how the Word is applied to their lives. For Christians, the end never justifies the means used to get there! We must be a people of integrity and good moral character if we are to be the light of the world that we are called to be.

Second, the strategy must be shaped by the vision. If it is not, there will be a lot of time and resources wasted that could have been put toward the fulfillment of the vision. For example, it would be foolish for a football coach to have his players practice shooting free-throws in the gym! Instead, he will spend every practice session developing the skills that each player will need to help his team be successful. Then, the coach will develop his game plans around his players' best abilities, both individually and as a team. This should also hold true for every leadership team. For example, if a team has a vision to train up future ministers, it would be foolish for the individual members of the team to go alone all over the world to preach and teach. Not that there is anything wrong with doing that, and occasionally there is no other option, but adopting that as a strategy would not be one that is shaped by the vision. However, if every member were to take a minister-in-training with him whenever possible when he traveled, and if he were to spend time mentoring him while on that trip, he would definitely be employing a strategy that would help fulfill the vision. [As a side note, this kind of inclusion of others who are not a part of the team should be done regularly by every leadership team. Nearly every strategy that a team embraces should include others who also embrace the vision and who have valuable gifts and talents that can be utilized and/or developed by being included. The more multi-faceted the vision is, the more complex the strategy will be, and the more participants it will require.]

Third, the strategy must be tailored to the situation. When I travel to the nations, I nearly always do a lot of teaching and preaching. On a recent trip to Asia, however, I was not permitted to teach or preach openly, but I was allowed to give words of greeting and encouragement to the churches I visited (as long as I was not standing behind the pulpit). I was also able to meet with pastors and leaders in more informal settings to share with them and to encourage them. Therefore, I adapted my usual strategy to fit the circumstances I encountered there. A strategy that works well with one group of people or in one geographic location may not work at all in another setting. That Paul understood and embraced this principle is evident in 1Corinthians 9:19-22 (NIV) where he writes, "Though I am free and belong to no one, I have made myself a slave to everyone, to win as many as possible. To the Jews I became like a Jew, to win the Jews. To those under the law I became like one under the law (though I myself am not under the law), so as to win those under the law. To those not having the law I became like one not having the law (though I am not free from God's law but am under Christ's law), so as to win those not having the law. To the weak I became weak, to win the weak. I have become all things to all people so that by all possible means I might save some."

Fourth, the strategy must be flexible. As the vision is being progressively revealed, the strategy must be re-evaluated with each new revelation. What was effective in the last season may not be effective in the current one. This does not mean that the old strategy was wrong, it simply means that the strategy must evolve along with the vision. For example, many ministries over the years have followed a mandate to see unsaved people come to Christ. There was a time in this nation when outdoor tent crusades were a very effective strategy that was used to implement that mandate. But the season has changed. Those ministries that still hold to this strategy (and there are some that do) are not seeing as many people saved in those meetings as they did in past years. In this season, most of the ministries that carry that mandate employ new strategies that are much more effective in this constantly-changing world in which we live. While it is a good idea for a leadership team to have strategies based upon one-year, three-year, five-year, and ten-year goals (and sometimes even longer), these goals and strategies should be regularly reviewed and adjusted as the vision develops and as the seasons change.

Finally, the strategy must be developed by seeking the leading of the Holy Spirit. Proverbs 14:12 (NIV) says, "There is a way that appears to be right, but in the end it leads to death." Just because a certain strategy looks good, it will not produce life if it is not what God wants. Strategies that come out of the think-tanks of human reasoning never accomplish the fullness of what God wants. Why? Because, as Paul writes in 1 Corinthians 2:12-14 (NIV), "What we have received is not the spirit of the world, but the Spirit who is from God, so that we may understand what God has freely given us. This is what we speak, not in words taught us by human wisdom but in words taught by the Spirit, explaining spiritual realities with Spirit-taught words. The person without the Spirit does not accept the things that come from the Spirit of God but considers them foolishness, and cannot understand them because they are discerned only through the Spirit." Then in Galatians 5:25 (NIV) he writes, "Since we live by the Spirit, let us keep in step with the Spirit." Strategy from the Holy Spirit will ALWAYS accomplish what is in the heart of the Father.

STRUCTURE

Structure is how the leadership team and the ministry it oversees function governmentally. The governing structure for the team is usually defined to some degree by the laws of the nation in which the team is based. However, the way the team members relate to each other, the recognition of who has authority in what areas, the methods of decision-making and delegating, and other such functions constitute the real structure of the team. Even as the human body needs a skeletal system to function as it should, a leadership team also needs a structure that all of its members freely and willingly embrace. And here, again, the formation of that structure must be led by the Holy Spirit. There is no "one size fits all" formula that works for every peer-level team. The teams that try to copy a structure that works well for another team discover, at some point, that it is not ideal for them. In fact, a structure that has been copied will most likely eventually quench what the Holy Spirit wants to accomplish with the team that does the copying. Why? Because cloning does not produce the life that is necessary for a team to be successful. Structure should never be used to try to produce life. Instead, the life that the Holy Spirit breathes into each team through its mandate and vision should beget the structure appropriate to that team. While different teams may have structures that are similar in some aspects, there will be other expressions of each team's structure that are different from the others. Why? Because the life that energizes each team will express itself somewhat differently in each one.

And like the vision, the values, and the strategy, the structure must also be allowed to change as necessary, because as those three change, the structure will sometimes have to change accordingly.

While it is essential that each of these foundation stones be laid according to what the Lord specifically desires for each individual leadership team, it is equally important that all of the members of the team be fully "on board" with all of them. If they are not, the purposes for which the Lord brought that team together will never be fully accomplished, and the team itself will eventually fall apart. Jesus said, "If a house is divided against itself, that house will not be able to stand" (Mark 3:25, NASB). However, if the proper foundation stones are in place, and if everyone on the team whole-heartedly embraces them, then its God-ordained purposes will be fulfilled in a far greater way than anyone can imagine! In His prayer for believers throughout the ages in John 17:20-23 (NIV) Jesus said, "My prayer is not for them alone. I pray also for those who will believe in me through their message, that all of them may be one, Father, just as you are in me and I am in you. May they also be in us so that the world may believe that you have sent me. I have given them the glory that you gave me, that they may be one as we are one—I in them and you in me—so that they may be brought to complete unity. Then the world will know that you sent me and have loved them even as you have loved me." The more we come into unity, especially in our leadership teams, the more the world will be impacted with the reality of who Jesus is!

Chapter 11
Putting it Together and Keeping it Together

When it comes to the makeup of a peer-level team (the people on the team) there is no single formula which, if followed, will guarantee success. However, there are some key guidelines that can be applied which will help define those individuals whom each team should include in order to accomplish God's purposes for it.

THE INITIAL FORMATION OF THE TEAM

As I stated previously, the person who will lead the team will receive a mandate and an initial vision. As he becomes convinced that these have been genuinely given to him by the Lord, and as he begins to speak about what he is hearing, the Holy Spirit will begin to draw others to him as they hear him share about the mandate and the vision. Why are they drawn? Usually, it is because they are hearing things that the Lord has already begun stirring in their own hearts. For several years before I knew anything about ICLC, the Lord had been speaking to me regarding five-fold ministry teams, but I did not know of anyone who was actually making the concept work in the way that I understood it. When I first heard about ICLC, all I knew was that it was a recently-formed fellowship of church leaders who seemed to be doing something significant in the Kingdom of God. So, I decided to attend one of their leadership conferences in Shawnee, Oklahoma, in order to check it out for myself. There were not too many in attendance at that meeting (1986, I believe), but I was so significantly touched by what I experienced there that I decided to attend their next conference. During a morning session in that subsequent meeting one of the leaders of ICLC shared about the mandate that God had given Sam Matthews to orchestrate a world-wide penetration of the Gospel, about the vision to train laborers to impact the nations, and about how the five-fold ministry team functioned that provided leadership to ICLC. As he spoke, my heart "burned within me" and I knew that I had found what I had been looking for. I then started attending every meeting possible, and I began to build a relationship with this group.

But the Holy Spirit also draws some for whom what is shared is a new concept. I know a brother who, upon listening to Sam as he ministered on the radio, was specifically led by the Lord to connect with Sam and build a relationship with him even though he had no desire to do so! In fact, he did not even like what he believed to be Sam's personality, but something about what Sam shared was drawing him. It is the mandate, expressed through the initial vision, which the Lord uses to draw other leaders.

However, not all of those who are attracted to the vision are being drawn together by the Holy Spirit. Therefore, it is critical, especially in the early stages of forming the team, to rely upon the leading of the Spirit as to who should be included. When God sent Samuel to Jesse's house to anoint a king from among his sons, Samuel thought that Eliab was probably going to be the one. But God told Samuel, "Do not look at his appearance or at the height of his stature, because I have rejected him; for God sees not as man sees, for man looks at the outward appearance, but the Lord looks at the heart" (1Samuel 16:7, NASB). Just because someone looks good, says the right things, and is apparently very gifted does not necessarily mean that person should be a part of the team. The key issue to be considered is what is in a person's heart, and only God knows for sure what that is. Therefore, the decision about the right ones to be a part of the initial team should be bathed in much prayer on the part of the one whom God has chosen to lead it.

Another thing that should be remembered is that there is strength in diversity. A person's natural tendency is to surround himself with those with whom he is most comfortable, and that often means people who have similar strengths, personalities, etc. As I stated earlier in this book, in my early years of pastoral ministry, I chose men to be my elders who were a lot like me in many ways. Even though we got along quite well with each other, I eventually discovered that we were so much alike that where we were strong we were even stronger together, but where we were weak we were tragically weak as a team. Paul makes it very clear in 1 Corinthians 12 that a variety of different parts make up a body (both physically and spiritually), and that all of them are necessary for it to function properly. A body cannot function if it is made up of only one part. Therefore, as the Holy Spirit gives direction as to who should be a part of the initial peer-level team, the leader must be willing to accept others who are different in their gifts, in their personalities, in their ministries, in their perspectives, etc. In this way, the team will be much more effective from its inception.

ADDING TO THE TEAM

In reality, adding to the team employs pretty much the same principles as those needed to form the team in the first place. Those to be added should have the same heart, they should have proven themselves loyal, and they should have gifts that are needed on the team. And once again, the leading of the Holy Spirit regarding whom to choose is critical! The main difference is that now all of the members of the team should be involved in the process of adding the new members.

PRUNING FROM THE TEAM

A member of a peer-level team should retain his position indefinitely. In order for a team to function well, it takes an undetermined amount of time for all the pieces to come together properly. Some members will take longer than others to feel comfortable on the team, to build strong relationships, and to reach their full potential. Therefore, there should be no "term limits" when it comes to how long a person serves as a member of the team. Besides, the relationships that develop on such a team are frequently as close as or closer than those in one's own natural family, and there are no "term limits" when it comes to family. But there are times when changes take place which will affect the way a family functions --- children grow up and move far away, a family member dies, etc. The same is true for peer-level teams, and this kind of pruning should be expected from time to time.

Occasionally, however, a team member will need to be removed from the team for more unpleasant reasons. There are two such reasons that are most frequently encountered. The first is due to ongoing, unrepentant sin. An offending member who has been approached in the manner described in a previous chapter yet still refuses to repent needs to be removed from the team. The other team members should support the decision to do so both privately and publicly so that no spirit of discord is allowed to grow either on the team or in the organization it oversees. The actual removal should be done in love and as graciously as possible, but it must be thorough --- a complete severing from the team --- so that his bad leaven does not begin to leaven the whole loaf, so to speak.

The second reason for removal is when a member has a change of heart regarding the mandate and the vision. When a member realizes that he is no longer in agreement, he will usually voluntarily remove himself. If he does not, he should be asked to leave so that he does not become contentious and divisive. If he is allowed to remain after it becomes apparent that his heart has changed, he will begin to negatively affect others on the team, whether he means to or not, and he will undermine the effectiveness of the team. I once had a couple come to me and tell me they were leaving the church. This came as no surprise because it had been obvious for some time that they were not "on board" with our mandate and vision. But I was shocked, angered, and saddened when they told me that they had only stayed as long as they had because they wanted to take as many church members as possible with them when they left! I should have dealt with the situation much earlier instead of waiting for them to come to me. Proverbs 6:16-19 (RSV) says, "There are six things which the LORD hates, seven which are an abomination to him: haughty eyes, a lying tongue, and hands that shed innocent blood, a heart that devises wicked plans, feet that make haste to run to evil, a false witness who breathes out lies, and a man who sows discord among brothers." Many scholars agree that because this scripture was written in this form, the seventh was considered to be the worst of all of them!

REPLACING THE TEAM LEADER

Although it should be a rare occurrence, it sometimes becomes necessary to select a new team leader. Hopefully, it will not be because of one of the reasons mentioned above, but that does occasionally happen. Normally, however, it is because the leader dies or because the Lord calls him to do something different. In either case, the new leader should be chosen very carefully, because he will be the key to what happens with the team in the future. Obviously, the same principles used to initially form a team should be applied here, but there are additional guidelines that should also be followed.

The first is that the leader who leaves properly, whether suddenly (such as death) or after much prayer and confirmation of the coming change, should already have been preparing another to take his place. A good leader will always be looking for and grooming his replacement, whether he plans to leave or not. When he does this under the leading of the Holy Spirit, things will continue to go forward properly after he leaves, much like what happened with Moses and Joshua and with Elijah and Elisha.

If the leader has not done this, then the rest of the team should not be in a hurry to choose his replacement. They should wait on God's timing. Just as cream rises to the surface, God's choice will become evident when He is ready to reveal it. This may happen quickly or it may take a while, but at some point it will become obvious to everyone who that person is to be.

The other thing that must be done is to invite and allow those to whom the former leader looked for oversight to be intimately involved in the selection of his replacement. In fact, if the former leader has not already made provision for his replacement, they should be the ones taking the lead in choosing that person. When they and the current team members are in agreement as to whom that should be, there will be a smooth transition.

Because God has a unique purpose for each team that He calls into existence, those whom He chooses to be a part of that team will also be unique. If He is allowed to put each team together the way He chooses to do so, then it will be properly equipped to accomplish those purposes!

Chapter 12

Where the Rubber Meets the Road

THE PEER-LEVEL TEAM IN THE LOCAL CHURCH

There are several applications for this type of team in the local church. The most obvious is in the context of the leadership team. I believe that a leadership team made up of Elders with the Senior Pastor (or whatever title he may carry) serving as the team leader is the best way to lead a church. And when this team functions as a peer-level team in the way that I have described it in this book, I believe it is the ideal form of leadership and oversight for a local church.

But I also believe that this concept should be applied to every area of the church's ministry. Quite often, ministry areas such as worship, youth, children, benevolence, deacons, and such are headed up by an individual. But what if each area were to operate under the leadership of a peer-level team instead of under the leadership of an individual, or even under a committee which simply serves as advisers to the leader? Should this happen, I believe that every ministry of the church would become much more effective in what it has been called to do. Also, many members of the church, some of whom were simply "attenders" before, would become involved in some area of ministry and begin to realize that they are an integral part of what the church is doing. They would begin to take personal ownership of their areas of responsibility, and the corporate vision would come alive in them. This is why, as much as is practically possible, the peer-level team concept should be applied to the Pastor and his Elders, to the Pastor and his staff, to each Elder and the team leaders he oversees, and to every area of ministry in the church.

THE PEER-LEVEL TEAM IN PARACHURCH MINISTRIES

Usually, ministries which operate outside of a local church's oversight or apart from an established denomination are governed by some kind of board of directors. Most of these boards are made up of people who genuinely have a heart for the ministry and honestly seek the Lord's guidance in their decisions regarding the ministry, therefore the ministry is productive and effective in many ways. Sometimes, however, the board operates much like those of secular organizations, and the ministry becomes more of a business than a Spirit-led ministry. Or sometimes, the board is simply a collection of yes-men who rubber-stamp every desire of the leader of the ministry. In these latter two scenarios, the ministry falls far short of what God's purposes are for that ministry.

Although any or all of the above examples may appear to be successful in what they are doing, probably none of them are truly successful in the eyes of God. You see, the success of a ministry should not be measured simply by what it has accomplished; instead, it should be evaluated by comparing what has been accomplished with the goals and plans that the Lord has for that ministry. And I believe that a parachurch ministry led by a peer-level leadership team will stand a much better chance of being seen as successful in God's eyes than any of the other styles of leadership.

THE APPLICATION OF THE PEER-LEVEL CONCEPT TO APOSTOLIC TEAMS

Even though the words apostle, prophet, evangelist, pastor, and teacher have been used in the church since its birth in the first century, the understanding (revelation, if you will) of Five-fold Ministry Teams, or Apostolic Teams, is a fairly new concept in the modern church. This is largely due to a realization that team leadership is more effective than individual leadership, and also due to a deeper revelation of the divine purpose for the existence of such a team. Paul spelled this out quite clearly in Ephesians 4:11-13 (NIV) where he wrote, "So Christ himself gave the apostles, the prophets, the evangelists, the pastors and teachers, to equip his people for works of service, so that the body of Christ may be built up until we all reach unity in the faith and in the knowledge of the Son of God and become mature, attaining to the whole measure of the fullness of Christ."

Although much could be said about these teams and what they do, my concern here is how they should function, and I believe that the peer-level leadership team concept is the best model for them to use. Unfortunately, many of these teams function differently and, consequently (in my opinion), are not as effective as they could be. The Apostolic Team of which I am a member functions, for the most part, as the kind of peer-level team that I have described in these pages. I believe that, largely because of this, the team has seen a lot of genuine success over the years --- it has accomplished much of what God has intended for it to do. I am convinced that the same will hold true for every Apostolic Team that functions as a peer-level leadership team in which an apostolic person is the leader, and the other members of the team represent all five of the Ephesians 4:11 ministries.

THE APPLICATION OF PEER-LEVEL TEAMS TO THE MARKETPLACE

Even though this book has been written from a clearly Christian perspective, I believe that the peer-level leadership team concept can work in any environment. It can be applied to large corporations, small businesses, government bureaucracies, civic organizations, non-profits, police forces, even the military. Imagine how much more effective each of these could be if it were led by a peer-level team. Divine principles bear good fruit regardless of where they are applied.

LAST WORDS
It's Not Just "Pie in the Sky"

In my personal experience, the peer-level leadership team concept is more than just a theory; I have seen it work first-hand, both in local churches and in an Apostolic Team setting. Has it worked perfectly all of the time? Of course not, and it most likely will not work perfectly all of the time in any given situation. Why? Because everyone involved is human, and humans are not perfect. But the more committed everyone is to making it work, the better it will function, and the more truly successful (according to God's definition of success) the team will become. However, the key word here is **commitment**. All of those involved must be committed to seeing it happen. If they are not, and especially if the leader of the team is not committed to it, it will fail. But when everyone makes a personal commitment to do everything possible to make it happen, what is produced will prove to be the best kind of leadership team any organization could hope for. In order to achieve the excellence that we all desire, we must raise the bar by pursuing this higher standard for team leadership!

ACKNOWLEDGEMENTS

This book would not have been written without the input and encouragement I received from others. My heartfelt thanks go out to Larry and Janet who encouraged me along the way and who served as my first proof-readers and informal editors. I also appreciate all those who encouraged me to keep writing. And of course I want to thank my family, especially my wife Cindy, for encouraging me and standing with me along the way. I could not have done it without you! But above all I want to thank the Lord for giving me the inspiration and grace to write this. May it affect many for His glory and for the expansion of His kingdom!

www.ingramcontent.com/pod-product-compliance
Lightning Source LLC
Chambersburg PA
CBHW030847180526
45163CB00004B/1476